The Little Apostle on Crutches

Written by Henriette Delamare

Illustrated by Anne Simoneau

Catholic Heritage Curricula
P. O. Box 579090, Modesto, CA 95357
1-800-490-7713 www.chcweb.com

The Little Apostle on Crutches was originally published by Benziger Brothers in 1911.

Illustrations and cover art by Anne Simoneau

Illustrations and special features © 1997

Distributed by Catholic Heritage Curricula
P.O. Box 579090, Modesto, CA 95357
1-800-490-7713 www.chcweb.com

ISBN: 978-0-9788376-7-9

Printed by Publishers' Graphics LLC
St. Louis, Missouri
August 2014
Print code: PGSTL00945

Contents

I   A Small Promoter   *page* 1

II   Willie's Business Venture   12

III   Poor Nancy's Trouble   22

IV   The Visit to the Doctor   32

V   Nancy's New Eyes   41

VI   A Day's Treat   48

VII   The Little Orphan   61

VIII   Willie's Revenge   70

IX   The Prodigal Son   78

X   A Surprise Party   86

XI   Baby's Day with Buddy   99

XII   The Two Portraits   113

XIII   A Holiday in the Country   119

XIV   Found at Last!   126

Chapter I
A Small Promoter

"I wonder you don't get discouraged of all your praying and church going, Mrs. Browne, for certainly the Lord doesn't seem to reward you for it! First you loses your husband, then your boy Bob, that ought to have been your support, runs away and leaves you, and the Lord knows what's become of him, then your gal Nancy, that used to be a cute little kid, seems to grow duller and more helpless every week, and to crown all, there's that poor mite, wee Willie, that's bright enough for anything, and a helpless cripple for life."

"Come, come, Mrs. Warner, it's not so bad as

*"I wonder you don't get discouraged of all your praying
and church going, Mrs. Browne, for certainly the
Lord doesn't seem to reward you for it!..."*

you make out," said Mrs. Browne as gently as she could, for her neighbor's ways and manners jarred upon her not a little. "My dear husband has left us, that's true, but he died a most beautiful and holy death. As for Bob, last time he wrote to me he said he had a good situation and hoped to send me money soon. Boys must be boys, and they're seldom good correspondents, but I know my lad's heart is in the right place. As for poor Nancy, she's a bit slow and clumsy, but there never was a more willing girl or a sweeter tempered one, and I expect she's just at the awkward age, that's all. So long as I can keep my health and work for them all, I've got no cause to complain. Besides which, even when the Lord does send me crosses, I know it's all for the best and out of love of me. 'Whom the Lord loveth, He chastiseth.' You know it says that in the Bible."

"I didn't think you Catholics held much account of the Bible, and in any case, if I were you, I'd wish the Lord didn't love me so much, if all your troubles is a sign of His love. There's wee Willie now!"

"Of course it's a cross to me to see the dear little fellow such a sufferer, but he's so brave and patient, and so cheery in spite of all, that it takes the bitterness out of even that sorrow. Besides which, the doctors have promised me that he will be cured before he grows to be a man."

"And you *believe* in doctors, Mrs. Browne?" said Mrs. Warner disdainfully.

"Yes, Mrs. Warner, and I believe in the goodness of God most of all, and if I have troubles I'll know where to go for help to bear them. Ah! here are my two youngest. They're well and strong enough anyhow. I've *that* to be thankful for," and hastily leaving her neighbor, Mrs. Browne went to meet the two pretty little girls, one a black-eyed baby of four, and her sister, a demure little girl of about six.

"That Mrs. Browne," exclaimed Mrs. Warner to the next neighbor she could catch hold of, "she fairly irritates me with her goodiness and her ways of saying all's for the best."

"Well, it's a heap better than always grumbling and growling over everything, as *some* people do," returned the other woman, determined to put an end to Mrs. Warner's well-known flow of grievances.

"Where's my wee Willie? Has anyone seen him?" asked Mrs. Browne as she entered her small but very neat cottage.

"Here, Mother!" answered a cheery voice accompanied by the sound of rapidly moving crutches as the child hurried forward to meet her with his ever-ready smile. Neither his face nor figure in any way denoted a deformed or crippled child. He was very slight, it is true, and small for a boy of nearly nine, but his oval face, with bright brown eyes, delicately chiseled features, and clear complexion, would in no way have led one to expect a sickly child. His cheeks, though rather thin, were fairly rosy, his back straight as an arrow, and his hands particularly well formed. Indeed, the only thing the matter with him was one poor helpless leg, thin and withered, which hung useless, heavily ironed on both sides. It always ached more or less and was at times very painful, but his mother had taught the little lad to bear his trouble with cheerful patience, and he was never known to complain or murmur at his inability to do as other children did.

For several months past, he could not even sit down, owing to the apparatus he wore, but had either to lie down or stand. This he felt a good deal, for it prevented his being able to attend school for many hours at a time.

He would go in for certain lessons, but although he could move about on his crutches with ease for hours at a time, he could not without pain and fatigue stand still for more than half an hour or so. Yet he loved to go to school, even if it were but for a short time, and the good Sisters were delighted to have him, for he was such a bright little pupil and gave such good example to the other children by his earnest piety, his love of work, and his polite manners.

"And what have you been doing, Willie?" inquired his mother, her face brightening as she looked into his frank, honest brown eyes.

"I went to school for a history lesson, Mother, then went round to look up a few of my associates, and since then I've been hurrying along helping Sis to get everything ready. All's just finished now, and you've only got to come in and sit down. I'm sure you must be tired and hungry after working all day."

"I can see who laid the cloth," said Mrs. Browne with a smile as she looked at the neatly dressed table with a big bunch of flowers in the center and a little bunch of violets laid by her own plate.

"Oh, we both did that," said Willie, who was always anxious that his sister should share in their mother's praise. "Here, Nancy, wait till I come and help you dish up," he added, hurrying back to the kitchen.

A few minutes afterward both the children came back, and with loving solicitude Willie helped his sister to place the dishes on the table and set them straight, a thing Nancy never could manage, much to her mother's annoyance.

The meal, though simple, was a plentiful one and very well prepared, and Mrs. Browne, who had been doing a hard day of washing and ironing, enjoyed it as fully as the children.

"And how about your associates, Willie?" she inquired, for she knew what pride and pleasure the child took in his office of Promoter*.

It was bright little Sister Teresa who had thought of this new plan of having boy Promoters. At first all the Promoters in the parish had been women, and, well—I can't say much for the zeal or energy these ladies put into their work. They had so much else to do—they did so *hate* to ask anybody to join, and when people had joined, they took no further interest in them, didn't care if they had their leaflets or anything.

"Why not have children Promoters?" said Sister Teresa. "I feel sure they'd do far better work for Our

---

* Promoter: a person who encouraged fellow parishioners to have more devotion to the Sacred Heart of Jesus through the Apostleship of Prayer. The Apostleship of Prayer (www.apostleshipofprayer.org) asks that one offers himself and his entire day as a prayer for the good of the whole world, that God's will be done on earth as it is in heaven. Associate: a fellow Promoter.

Lord. There's wee Willie, for instance. That child wouldn't be afraid to ask the President if he met him."

"I think it's a very good idea," said Father Burton. So half a dozen children were enrolled and did fine work, especially the boys, under the acknowledged leadership of Willie.

"Do you know, Mother," said the little lad, "I've got a new associate today! You'll never guess who he is."

"Won't I? Then he must be somebody very unlikely. Not Mr. Grosse, anyhow," she said, laughing. Mr. Grosse was a man of wealth who came to church in his auto and was regarded with great awe by most of the congregation.

"How did you guess, Mother? Yes, it is Mr. Grosse."

"You don't mean to say you had the—well, the nerve to go up and ask him to join?"

"Well, I wasn't asking a favor for myself, was I?" said Willie apologetically. "I met him in the street and I asked him very politely. He seemed rather astonished at first, but after a minute he said, 'Certainly, my boy, you can put my name down,' then he laughed and said, 'You're a mighty small Promoter.' 'Well, sir,' I said, 'I'm not very big, but Father Burton says one's never too small to begin to work for the Sacred Heart,' and he patted me on the shoulder and said: 'Quite right, my little lad, work on, and never be ashamed of your Faith. Too many people *are* nowadays.' So you see he wasn't so stern and haughty as people say."

"No, I'm glad you asked him," said Mrs. Browne. "I expect he must be rather lonely in that great house, with no children to cheer it up," and she looked round with a loving smile at her four grouped round the table.

Just then a man came to the door and asked to speak to her on important business. Mrs. Browne was away quite a long time, and when she returned her usual happy smile had vanished and she looked pale and anxious.

Willie had noticed it in a minute, but he said nothing until he had helped Nancy to carry the dinner things to the kitchen and settled the two little ones to a game in the other room. Then he came and leaned against his mother, putting one arm lovingly around her neck.

"What is it, Mother dear? Tell your Willie."

Oddly enough Willie was the only one of her children to whom Mrs. Browne ever confided her troubles, but he was not only sympathetic, but so strangely reasonable and thoughtful for a child that she always felt comfort in talking things over with him, besides which, she knew she could trust him never to repeat anything she had said.

"Oh, Willie!" she said with a sob, "you know that restaurant I've worked so hard for?"

"Yes, Mother dear, and they always paid rather shabbily."

"Well, yes, and worse than that, they are now owing me over five weeks' salary and had promised faithfully to pay it tomorrow, and now that man has come to tell me they've gone bankrupt and shut up the place, and I'm not likely to get a cent for ever so long, and very little then. Oh, dear!" she added, bursting into tears, "and I worked so hard for that money and was reckoning on it to pay the rent, and now what shall I do?"

"Don't cry, Mother," he said, kissing her tenderly, "it may not be so bad as the man says, or even if it is, wouldn't the landlord wait a little while?"

"No, that's just it; he's such a hard man!"

"Couldn't we write to Bob?"

"No, he has never given me the address of his last place," said the mother with a bitter sigh.

"Anyhow, I'm sure Father Burton would lend you the money, Mother."

"I hate to ask him—" she began.

"Oh, no, you needn't mind, because we're sure to be able to pay him back soon. I'll just set myself thinking hard how I can earn some money for you, Mother."

"You! Poor wee Willie!"

"Don't you trouble, Mother dear. I'll manage it somehow," said the little lad brightly. "There's the bell ringing for the May services. Won't you come with me, dear? You'll feel ever so much better afterward, and good old Nancy will put the little ones to bed while we're gone."

Chapter II
Willie's Business
Venture

"Hullo, poor Kiddy, is your leg troubling you to-day? It isn't often one sees you with such a solemn face," said one of his fellow Promoters when he met Willie on the street the next morning.

"No, it isn't my leg this time. It's because I'm feeling bad, because I can't think of any way to earn money for mother and the girls, and now that Bob's away it comes ever so hard on poor mother to have to do all the earning for the lot of us. I can run errands, and I can knit socks, but one earns so very little at those."

"Well, you're such a clever little chap I feel sure

you ought to be able to earn plenty, if we could only think how," answered his friend Herbert. "Don't you trouble, though, Willie. I'll think it over, and when I see you again at noon, on my way home from school, I feel sure I shall have an idea."

The Sister thought Herbert very stupid and inattentive that morning, but she was fairly startled when he jumped up and clapped his hands, exclaiming, "Hurrah! I've got it!" "Got what, Herbert?" she inquired sternly. "Oh, Sister, I'll tell you after school. I think it will be just splendid!" "Well, it will be very different from what your work has been this morning then," she answered, but Herbert was generally such an excellent pupil that she felt sure he would be able to give her some good excuse for his conduct.

On the way home he rushed up to Willie, who had come to meet him, and exclaimed:

"Willie lad, I've got it! I wonder why I didn't think of it before. You could sell papers on the street. The boys get quite a lot at that. I'm chummy with a chap who is boss of one of the best corners in town, and I'm sure he'd give you a helping hand, and Father knows people both on the "News" and on the "Times," and they'd be kind to you, and I've spoken about it to Sister, and she thinks it might be a very good thing," panted Herbert, who had poured all this out without even taking a breath.

"Yes, I think it's a fine idea," said Willie, "but I wonder if I could run as fast as the other boys and jump on the cars and all that? I don't think Mother'd let me."

"No, of course you could not do all that. But you could just go about on the sidewalk and sell to the passersby, and Sister thinks people would soon get to know you and favor you, just because you can't rough it like the others."

"Well, thanks ever so much, Herbert. I'll talk to Mother about it. She'll be in soon."

"All right, and I'll come in and see you on my way home from afternoon school, and if you like I'll take you round to introduce you so you can begin work tomorrow."

Mrs. Browne was very loath to consent to the arrangement, but she saw the little lad's heart was so set on it that she called on the doctor to ask his advice on the matter. His answer was that it would be the best thing in the world for the child, as it would keep him in the open air, give him plenty of exercise, and something to interest him, besides which, the fact of being out in all weathers must strengthen his constitution, and that was what they were specially aiming at. Still, of course, he must not overdo it—say two hours in the morning and two in the evening would be sufficient. The doctor kindly added that he would patronize the little chap himself and tell many of his gentlemen friends about him.

So Mrs. Browne very reluctantly gave her consent on condition that Willie should avoid contracting any of the rough habits of some of the more vulgar boys, and should promise faithfully to keep to the sidewalk, also that he should not stay longer than the appointed hours and should promise to study between times.

The very next morning there was a new newsboy at the corner of the street, and as he skipped about quickly on his crutches his cheery voice rang out clear as a silver bell, "Paper, sir? Terrible accident! Latest telegrams! 'Times' or 'News,' sir?" and many were the hurrying business men who stopped to buy a paper of the sweet faced little lad who so bravely kept his own on his crutches.

"Never mind the change—haven't time," shouted one or two who had dropped a dime into his hand, and when he got home that morning, a little after nine o'clock, he was very tired, it is true, but the proud bearer of sixty-five cents profit. What a joy for his mother when she came home and how happy he was to think that he was at last earning something toward supporting the family!

Mrs. Browne had thought he might get tired of this work after a while, but no, he went bravely on day after day, and yet none of his other duties suffered for it, nor did he contract any undesirable friendships or habits from the other newsboys. His nature was too refined, his knowledge of right and wrong too clear, and his conscience too pure to be sullied by what went on around him. He always wore his badge of the Sacred Heart pinned inside his little blouse, and if he heard any coarse or profane words he would instantly offer up a prayer.

On the whole, the other boys, even if they didn't like him, respected and rather admired the plucky little fellow who worked so hard in spite of being a cripple. Unconsciously, he even had a softening and uplifting effect on many of them, for they felt ashamed at times to be rough or coarse or quarrelsome under the gaze of those pure, earnest brown eyes. Even Sammy, the roughest boy, was better behaved when near the "poor little Kiddo," to whom he was such a funny contrast.

Things had gone quite uneventfully for several months when, one misty, slippery morning, a gentleman who had bought a two-cent paper paid the little lad in pennies, then hurried to his train, which was standing at the corner with passengers piling in.

Just as the child was about to slip the coins into his pocket, he was attracted by the brightness of one of them, and found it to be a five-dollar gold piece which the gentleman had given him by mistake.

Some of the boys might have pocketed it with glee. Not so our honest little Willie. He started to run after the gentleman, shouting and hurrying along. Forgetful of everything but his anxiety to restore the coin to its owner, he had made a step or two on the road and stood waving the gold piece with one hand, while with the other he had put his crutch out a good step ahead of him and was steadying himself on it. Just then an automobile came rushing by, utterly regardless of the crowd in the street. Barely missing two women who were attempting to get into the streetcar, it struck the little cripple's crutch and smashed it to pieces.

The onlookers gave a cry of horror, expecting to see the poor child crushed to death, but, as if by a miracle, he fell and rolled away from the machine to-

Barely missing two women who were attempting to get into the streetcar, it struck the little cripple's crutch and smashed it to pieces.

ward the curbstone, still clutching the gold piece in his hand. Loving hands picked him up and he was helped into a nearby drugstore while a burly policeman, who had seen the whole proceeding, endeavored to stop the automobile. With a mocking shout its occupants drove on, but not before several of the incensed bystanders had taken down its number. "And I'll have that auto traced and them people made to pay for their conduct if I have to pursue them till doomsday," exclaimed the enraged policeman.

"Are you hurt, dear?" asked one of those who had followed the child into the store, where he was crying bitterly at the thought of his broken crutch.

"Oh, no, ma'am. I don't think I'm much hurt, but I was trying so hard to earn money for Mother, and now she'll have to buy me a new crutch!" said Willie, trying to swallow down his tears.

" 'Deed and that she won't," cried the policeman, who had just come in. "I'll see to your having one given to you by those people and something more than that, too. The big hulking brutes! It wasn't enough for 'em to drive among a lot of women. They would have cheerfully run down this poor little cripple!"

"Where did your mother buy your crutches, son,

do you know?" asked a kind faced gentleman.

"It was at Albright Brothers' Drugstore, sir. They've lots of them there, but that's at Grant Street, right the other side of town."

"Never mind, little chap. We'll get you into my auto, then I'll soon drive there and make matters straight for you."

So, as soon as the doctor who had been called had ascertained that the child was in no way hurt, but only a bit shaken, Willie was taken off to Albright Brothers, where the gentleman bought him a fine new crutch.

He was now only anxious at the thought of what his mother would say as to his disobedience. She was terribly upset at first, and it was only after Father Burton had made her see that this accident might just as well have happened when Willie was running an errand or even walking to church, that she finally yielded to Willie's tears and entreaties and allowed him to take up his work again.

For the first few weeks she suffered agonies of apprehension, until one Sunday she talked about this to the gentle, sympathetic Sister Superior.

"Do you think you ought to worry like this?" said the latter in her gentle voice. "Does it not seem a lack of confidence in God? Surely our dear Lord can and will protect His faithful little apostle. Everyone says his escape from that auto was nothing short of miraculous. Why should you think this protection from above should fail him another time?"

The mother felt the truth of these remarks, and henceforth she ceased from troubling, leaving her darling child in God's hands with loving confidence.

Chapter III
Poor Nancy's Trouble

"Whaken Willie took up his stand for the first time after his accident he met with quite an ovation, not only from the boys and his regular customers, but from many who had never noticed him before. He never thought he had so many friends. Indeed, he really had made many new ones, among whom was the burly policeman.

"Hullo, little Kiddy! Feeling all right again?" he asked kindly.

"Fine and dandy, thank you, sir, and I've got a nice new crutch, you see."

"Good! and you'll have something else besides,

I bet, for we caught them folks and they'll be made to give you something, for sure. How did you come to be out on the road, though? I'd noticed you never left the sidewalk, which is far safer for a little cripple like you."

Then Willie told him the story of his five-dollar piece, which, even in his fall, he had still clutched in his hand and which he now carried in his pocket, safely wrapped up in paper in the hopes of seeing the gentleman some day.

"Well, you're an honest little chap, for sure," said the policeman. "It's too bad you should have got such a scare just when you was doing the right thing. But you won't be the one that'll get the worst of that accident, sure as my name's Patrick Murphy."

"Oh, is it?" said Willie with a beaming smile. "I'm so glad."

"Glad! Why, Kiddy?"

"Well, because you must be an Irishman, and if you're an Irishman then I expect you're a Catholic."

"Are *you* one? Well, I might have guessed it. Yes, I'm a kind of a sort of a Catholic, not much of a one to boast of, but I've got a dear old mother praying hard for me over there in the old country."

"Then I'm sure she'd like you to join the Apostleship of Prayer. You've nothing to do but just say the offering every morning. Here, I'll give you a leaflet and you can just read all about it. I'm a Promoter."

"All right, little Kiddy, I'll think it over," said Pat Murphy good-naturedly, as he tucked the leaflet into his pocket and hurried off to his post again.

It was over two weeks later that Willie joyfully recognized the gentleman who had given him the five dollars and hurried after him to return it. He had heard of Willie's adventure, however, and nothing could persuade him to take it back, so Willie gave it to his mother, and it helped to pay Father Burton the rent he had advanced for them.

The rush of business had been over sooner than usual one day, and as Willie leaned up against the corner store he began to read a column in one of the papers he had in his hand. It happened to be an article on the care of children's eyesight, and told how many boys and girls, who were thought to be dull or awkward, were only troubled with deficient sight, which, if not attended to, might eventually lead to total blindness. It was as a ray of light to the boy, explaining so perfectly the unaccountable change in his sister.

Just then he stopped to sell a paper to a regular

customer of his, a tall, stately looking man with a rather sad expression. Though he took his "Times" every morning from Willie and always paid him a nickel and refused the two cents change with a wave of the hand, he appeared in too much of a hurry ever to stop and speak to the little lad as so many people did.

He had just passed on, across the street, when Willie heard two ladies who were waiting for a car talking about him.

"You see that handsome man who has just crossed the road?" said one. "That's Doctor Ferris, the great eye specialist, who used to be in Chicago."

"Yes? How did he come out West, I wonder? I seem to have heard some story connected with him."

"Why, yes, don't you know! He is the one whose wife suddenly left him, taking their child with her. It appears she was very quick-tempered, and they had a quarrel about some silly thing. She said she'd leave him, but he never thought she meant it. He went out on a case, and when he got back both she and the child were gone. He tried every means to find them again, but they seemed to have vanished completely. That's why after a time he came out here, to try to forget. Sad, isn't it? And they say he's a charming fellow."

"Does he live near here?"

"Yes, just two blocks down Lincoln Street. Here! Hurry! There's our car."

And the ladies went off, leaving Willie full of hopes and plans. Surely it was God who had caused him to see that article and hear of this doctor on one and the same day! He must see what he could do for poor Nancy.

When he got home that evening he hoped to have a talk with his mother before dinner, but she came in at the very last minute and was in a hurry to sit down and eat, as she had to hasten out to some customers as soon as the meal was over.

Nancy, poor girl, was nervous from having to hurry, and as she was bringing in two dishes at a time, she endeavored to put one down on the table, and placed it so much over the edge that it fell to the ground, spilling all the contents on the rug.

For once the gentle Mrs. Browne was very angry and scolded Nancy severely for her carelessness, and the poor girl burst into an uncontrollable fit of crying and sobbing, which still further annoyed her mother.

"Oh, *please*, Mother, don't scold Nancy. I'm sure she can't help it. I read—" began Willie,

Surely it was God who caused him to see that article and hear of this doctor on one and the same day! He must see what he could do for poor Nancy.

"And please, Willie, mind your own business," said his mother severely. "You are growing much too conceited and bossy. You have no right to interfere when I find fault with one of your sisters. Do you suppose you know better than your own mother?"

Willie never answered a word, but did his best to help in repairing the disaster, and the usually cheery meal passed gloomily.

As soon as she got up from table Mrs. Browne hurried out to her customers, and Willie helped his sister to wash up the dishes, straighten the rooms and put the little ones to bed, closely watching her all the time and feeling more and more convinced that the girl's sight was defective.

He always had to go to bed by eight o'clock, as the doctor insisted on many hours of lying on his back, and he had to rise quite early on account of his papers. Before going upstairs that evening, however, he tried to comfort and cheer his sister, and after some time he heard her come up into her own room, which was next to his.

His mother had returned, and evidently some friend had come with her, for he could hear voices in the parlor. Soon, however, another sound reached his ears even more distinctly, and that was the sound of Nancy's heartbroken sobs. After a while he could stand it no longer and rapped on the wall, which was always the signal that he wanted her. The girl came almost instantly, and trying to steady her voice, she asked anxiously:

"Are you sick, Brother? Do you want anything?"

"Yes, I want you, Sis. Come and kneel here by my bed so that I can talk to you—." Then putting his arm round his sister's neck and drawing her close to him, he said tenderly, "Sis, tell me all about it. Is it because you can't see well?"

Nancy gave a low cry of pain.

"Oh, yes, Willie! How did you guess it? Oh, Willie," she exclaimed, bursting into a paroxysm of tears, "I think I'm going blind!"

"Hush, Sis, hush! Mother will hear you. Don't be afraid. It isn't as bad as all that. I read in a paper today that lots of children are like you and that it can be cured. What is it like?"

"Why, everything goes blurry and then things have two or three edges and they dance about and I can't tell which is the right one."

"That's it! That's it!" cried Willie. "Just what I was reading about, and I know a great eye doctor, and I'll take you to him and he's bound to cure you. Don't

cry any more, dear. I'm sure that's ever so bad for
your eyes. We'll pray hard to the Sacred Heart of Jesus. I know you'll be all right, dear Sis." And so the
little cripple boy, who knew so well what suffering
was, soothed and comforted his big sister. Before
she left him that night her heartbreaking sorrow had
changed to confident hope.

Still Willie did not go to sleep, for he lay listening
for the loved step of the mother, who never went to
bed until she had been round to kiss and bless her
children. She was astonished to find the boy awake
so late, and feared he must be sick, but when he got
her by his side he threw his arms around her, and
with wonderful tact for so small a child broke as gently as he could the ill news about Nancy's eyes.

"And to think I've been scolding the poor child for
it!" cried the mother. "But why in the world didn't
she tell me about her sight?"

"She was always hoping it would grow better. She
didn't like even to speak of it, it seemed to make it
more true, she said."

"Oh, dear! Oh, dear! One child a cripple, the other
going blind!" moaned the mother.

"Now, Mother, don't worry about it," said Willie
cheerfully. "I know a great eye doctor and I'll take

her to him."

"*You* know a great eye doctor, Willie?"

"Yes, he's one of my regular customers."

"Do you mean Dr. Ferris? But, child, he's ever so expensive. We could never afford to go to him."

"I mean Nancy to have the very best," said Willie in his quiet way, "and I've got a little money of my own, Mother. I'll manage it, don't you trouble."

Mrs. Browne knew that the child had a winning way, which generally made people willing to help him. Still, she hardly dared to hope that so great and busy a man as Dr. Ferris would interest himself in poor folk like themselves.

After leaving Willie she went into poor Nancy's room, but found the girl fast asleep. The child's face showed traces of her long fit of weeping.

Mrs. Browne passed a wretched night, reproaching herself with not having better watched over her child, and regretting every harsh word she had ever said to her about her clumsiness. She grieved, too, over the future, wondering if the child's eyes could be saved, and it was not till far into the night that the poor worn-out woman fell asleep.

Chapter IV
The Visit to the Doctor

Willie had felt very brave beforehand about stopping the great doctor, but his heart beat very painfully as he watched him come out of the barber's, a few doors farther down, and come rapidly toward him.

The child held his paper very tightly so as to detain him a little while. Looking him well in the face with those pleading brown eyes of his, he said:

"Please, sir, could I call and have a talk with you some time today? I have something *very* important that I want to ask you about."

At first the doctor seemed too surprised to answer,

then with a pleasant smile he said:

"Well, I haven't a minute free all day, but I could see you in the evening. What time could you come?"

"I leave here at six, sir. I could be at your house by ten minutes past, if that wouldn't be your dinner-time."

"No, that'll be all right. I'll expect you. Don't be later, if you can help it," and the doctor hurried off, forgetting to pay for his paper.

That evening Dr. Ferris heard the hurrying sound of the little crutches, and a minute later Willie was standing before him, his cap in his hand and his pretty wavy brown hair brushed well off his forehead.

"Well, my little man, what is it? Won't you sit down?" asked the doctor.

"You'll have to excuse me, please, sir, because I can't sit down on account of my irons, but I can lean *so* on my crutches, if you don't mind," and without the slightest hesitation he told his story to the doctor, explaining how the newspaper article had first given him the idea of his sister's eye trouble, and how he had heard the ladies say that Dr. Ferris was the great eye specialist, and had determined his sister should have the very best advice, if he could manage it, because, he added in his quaintly old-fashioned way, "I think a lot of those cheap doctors often do you more harm than good."

Dr. Ferris smiled.

"Only, sir," continued Willie rather anxiously, "I must tell you we're very poor folk. Father's dead and my brother Bob, has gone away, we don't know where, and of course I have to help Mother and take care of the girls the best I can. The worst of it is I'm only a little chap and a cripple too, but," he added cheerily, "I can do a lot of things in spite of that."

"I see you can," said the doctor. "I thought the money you got for the papers was just for your own pleasures."

"Bless you, no," said Willie with a laugh. "I turn it all in to Mother and it goes to pay the rent and the little ones' schooling and lots of things. But Mother gives me a little out of it every week, only I generally spend some of it on a few toys and sweets for the little kiddies, or a surprise for Mother or Nancy. Of course I didn't know we'd have this expense or I'd have saved up. Still I have the ten dollars the people in the auto gave me for nearly running over me. Would that do?"

"That'll be plenty," said the doctor, "perhaps more than enough."

"See," said Willie, with his bright smile, "how things always turn out for the best! I was so scared when my crutch was broken and I was afraid I was going to fall under that auto, and I little thought that fall was going to bring me just the money I would need for poor Sis's eyes. If that isn't enough, sir, I might work it out in some way or pay you by degrees, or Mother might do some washing for you. She gets up shirt fronts splendidly!"

"Does she? Then I should be very glad to employ her, for mine have been done very badly of late. Your mother and you must find it rather hard at times to make both ends meet, I should think. Do you not?"

"Yes, at times, but you see, sir, we're Catholics and that helps one so much, doesn't it? It keeps one contented and happy—and teaches one to bear one's troubles."

"Does it?" said the doctor rather dreamily. "Well, I suppose it *ought* to," he added. "Now then, my little friend, bring me your sister tomorrow at nine precisely and I'll see what we can do for her. There," he added, opening the door into a dining-room in which dinner was laid and taking some beautiful fruit from a dish, "perhaps you would like to take some of these home with you."

"Oh, thank you, sir!" exclaimed the child, his face beaming with pleasure. "That will be a lovely surprise for Mother and the girls."

As the doctor watched the child hurrying down the street he murmured:

"Bless his loving little heart! Does that child ever think of himself, I wonder? Only nine years old—and crippled—and tells one with a beaming smile that he has to help mother and look after the girls! 'Being a Catholic helps one so, and teaches one to bear one's troubles!' Why haven't I let it help me bear mine? Ah! little Willie! You've taught me a lesson that's worth more to me than all the fees the rich folk give me. Courage and contentment under difficulties—a brave heart, an utter freedom from false shame where duty is concerned, a thoughtful love for others! With God's help I'll profit by his example."

The next morning exactly at nine the two children entered the doctor's waiting-room, which was already full of stylishly dressed ladies and wealthy men. Poor Nancy felt terribly nervous and was much relieved when, after a short time, a servant opened the door and called out, "Miss Browne, by appointment," then ushered them into the doctor's consulting room.

He greeted the children kindly and looked pityingly into poor Nancy's dull blue eyes and anxious face.

"Don't be frightened, little girl," he said gently, "and above everything don't cry. I will have to examine your eyes long and carefully and it will at times be trying and perhaps painful, but you must endeavor to be patient."

"Oh, sir, I'll be patient, and I'll try and do anything you tell me, but I'm dreadfully stupid," said poor Nancy humbly.

The doctor smiled. "You have seemed stupid because you could not see properly, but I'm sure that will soon be remedied. Now come with me into the other room, and don't be afraid."

"May Willie stand by me?" asked Nancy.

"Yes—on condition he neither moves nor speaks." And through the long examination Nancy underwent her brother stood with his hand protectingly on her arm and neither of the children uttered a syllable unless spoken to.

"Well, you're made of the same stuff as your brother, I see," said the doctor with a smile when he had concluded his tests. "I've rarely met with a more enduring patient. Now come back into the other room and we'll talk this matter over."

"Oh, please, sir!" said Nancy, vainly trying to keep

the tears out of her eyes, "don't tell me I'm going blind!"

"No, we can save your eyes now. But it was high time they should be seen to, and if your brother had not discovered your trouble, in a few months more you would have been past cure. It is always a great mistake not to speak of these things, Nancy," said the doctor while he waited for an answer from the telephone.

"Yes, and it was just by chance I happened to have time to look at the paper that day and saw the article," exclaimed Willie.

"Mighty good subject to have an article about," said the doctor. "It's a pity they don't have more such, instead of all the murders—yes—hello—by Monday evening, without fail? No, *this* evening. I must have them, it's very important. What time do you go to Mass tomorrow, children?"

"We always go to nine o'clock Mass and then Sunday school," answered Willie. "It gives me time to go round with my papers to regular customers before Mass."

"Well, that'll be all right. Come around and see me directly after Sunday school. I don't receive patients on Sunday generally, but I'll make an exception for you, because I want Nancy to get her glasses as soon as possible. Oh, by the by, here is a little bottle and a dropper. I want someone, your mother, perhaps, to put two drops in each eye night and morning."

"Please, sir, I think I better do it, because Mother is often in such a hurry of a morning, and in the evening her hands are often rather shaky with washing and ironing all day. Might I do it once here for you, to see if I do it right?"

"Certainly," said the doctor. "Nancy, kneel before your brother and throw your head well back and hold the lids of your eyes well apart while Willie drops the wash in."

And the doctor thought he'd rarely seen a more touching picture than that of the big, overgrown girl kneeling so confidingly before the little cripple, who, with contracted brow and compressed lips, carefully put the two drops in each of the poor weak eyes.

"Capital! that's perfectly well done. Do it again to-night and in the morning and don't fail to come to-morrow after Sunday school."

That Saturday evening the doctor looked at his watch after dinner.

"A quarter to seven—my appointment isn't till

eight. There's sure to be someone there—anyhow, I'll try it—"

Half an hour later a lady kneeling in church whispered to her neighbor:

"Look! there's the great Dr. Ferris going into the confessional! Did you know he was a Catholic?"

As Dr. Ferris walked on to his appointment he thought: Willie was right! It helps one and teaches one to bear one's troubles. I must never stay away so long again."

Chapter V
Nancy's New Eyes

T he next morning when the two entered the doctor's office Nancy hardly looked like the same girl as the poor timid child who had stood there the day before, trembling under the apprehension of a terrible calamity.

She was not exactly beautiful, but she had very pretty fluffy fair hair, with glints of gold. Her complexion was good, and there was a sweet, patient expression on her face, which was very touching to anyone who knew what she must have been going through for many long, weary months. The look of dull apathy which had made people think her stupid had vanished today, however, and given place to one of eager hope.

After greeting the children kindly, the doctor took a pair of spectacles from the table and bade the eager Nancy put them on.

"Now look about the room and tell me how you see with them," he added.

"Oh, sir!" cried Nancy, clasping her hands with delight, "I see! I can see everything, everything! Just as clear and straight! Oh, how good God has been to hear my prayers! How can I thank you, sir?"

"I think you ought rather to thank your little brother, for if it had not been for him I never could have helped you."

"Oh, I'm ever so grateful to Willie, sir. He always was the dearest little brother in the world. Still, he's my brother and you did not even know us! I can never be grateful enough to you."

"I'm very glad to have been able to help you so much, Nancy, and I hope—if you will faithfully follow my orders—to be able to cure you completely in time. Always remember I did it for the sake of my little friend, Willie."

Nancy turned her swimming eyes to her brother, threw her arms about his neck, and kissed him. Sud-

"O, sir!" cried Nancy, clasping her hands with delight, "I see! I can see everything! Just as clear and straight! Oh, how good God has been to hear my prayers! How can I thank you, sir?"

denly remembering where she was, she hastily sprang to her feet and apologized.

"That's all right, dear, quite natural and proper," answered the doctor, who felt his own eyes rather moist.

"Please, sir, I want to pay you all I can so far," said Willie in his business-like way. "I know what I've got couldn't nearly pay for all we owe you, but I took it out of the Savings Bank yesterday, and there's $14.84 to begin with, and if you'll allow me, I'll work out the rest. I'd sooner do all myself, if I could, because Mother has so many other calls for her money."

"How long did it take you to save this up, Willie?"

"Oh! Ever since I started work, and then there was my accident, you know."

Again the doctor found it necessary to brush something from his eyes.

"Look here, Willie," he said at last, "you know I told you the ten dollars would be more than enough. Indeed, if you'd let me, I'd rather not charge you any-thing." Then, seeing an anxious look on the child's face, he added, "Still, as I know you'd like to feel you had yourself paid for your sister's cure, if you like, I will take five dollars."

"That seems very little, sir."

"That's all I'll take. Remember, you're a personal friend of mine now. We never charge our friends what we charge other people, you know."

Willie's face glowed with pride.

"You're ever, ever so kind, sir, and I'm ever so proud to be your little friend. You must let me do things for you whenever I can. I'd always love to do anything in the world for you, sir!"

"I'm sure you would, and I daresay I'll often want you to help me in many ways."

"I know what I could do," exclaimed Willie joyfully. "I could knit you some socks. I can knit beautifully."

"Oh, that he can!" exclaimed Nancy.

"Well, you may knit me a pair of socks. I shall like them very much, I'm sure."

"What color would you like, sir?"

"Any color you prefer. I wish you to choose."

"And what size do you wear, sir? I could guess pretty well. Still, you might just as well have them fit perfectly."

"Just so, practical as ever, Willie!" laughed the doctor. "I wear tens."

"All right, sir, you'll have them by next Sunday."

"But I don't want you to be working at them when

you're tired."

"All right, sir. I do it when I'm on my back, you know. I have to lie down a certain number of hours, so I may just as well fill up the time. It's tedious work lying there doing nothing but thinking, though thinking and praying help a lot, too, don't they?"

"Yes, ever so much."

"And please, sir, Mother said she would so like to come and thank you this afternoon, if it wouldn't be intruding."

"Certainly not, I want to see her and explain many things about Nancy's eyes, and besides, I wish to speak to her about my shirt fronts. Oh, don't be anxious! That is in no way to be in payment for my professional services to your sister. You and I are to settle that between us. It is an understood thing, and while I think of it I'll give you a receipt for that five dollars."

"I wish I could do something for you, too," began Nancy.

"No knitting for you, mind!" said the doctor, "and very little needlework or reading."

"All right, sir," said Nancy with a smile, "but I might say some rosaries for you, perhaps. I'll say my rosary every day for you for a month at least."

"Thank you, Nancy. I shall be very grateful for that. Say it for my special intention."

"I'll say one, too!" exclaimed Willie.

"Thank you, Willie. Now tell your mother I'll be at home this afternoon between one and two, and here's some fruit for you to take home to the little kiddies."

I need hardly tell you how relieved and overjoyed the mother was when the children got home and Nancy, wild with joy, told her of the wonderful success of her spectacles. The girl was no longer dull and clumsy now, but went merrily about her work, singing like a bird about the house in the lightness of her heart. As time went on, her dull, lusterless eyes became almost as bright and sparkling as Willie's brown ones, and there was not a happier girl in all the town than Nancy.

Chapter VI
A Day's Treat

All the choir boys and Promoters were in a state of wild excitement, for Father Burton had promised to take them out for a day's treat, and when the kind priest did these things he always made it a most delightful time for the children, sparing neither trouble nor expense.

He had not as yet told them where they were going, and many were the guesses and suggestions made by one or other of the boys. A sail on the bay, a picnic in a canyon, a trip to the mountains, were all thought of, and their various advantages hotly upheld by those who had proposed them.

"Why, Willie!" exclaimed Herbert, looking at his friend's rather sober face, "You don't seem one bit excited about this treat. I think we'll have just lots of fun. We always have a grand time when we go out with Father."

"Yes," said Willie soberly, "and I hope you'll enjoy yourselves ever so much this year, but I don't think I can go. I wish I could."

"Not go! Why of course you'll go. You're one of the Promoters—the very best of them, too, for nobody has such a long list of associates as you have, Willie."

"It isn't that," answered Willie. "I know Father'll be kind enough to ask me, but I don't think I should leave my corner for a whole day just now. There's a chap that's been trying for weeks to get my place there, and if once he managed to do it—well—it would be bad for my business," added Willie.

"Why, that's too bad. Why don't you speak to Patrick Murphy about it?" asked Herbert.

"Well, I don't like to. It seems like telling tales and trying to get someone into trouble."

Herbert said no more to Willie, but determined to try and help him.

The next morning the coarse-spoken, rough lad

who had been annoying Willie for several weeks came up and jostled him so roughly that Willie nearly tripped and dropped the papers he was carrying into the gutter, then hurried round the corner with insulting words and a mocking laugh. To his surprise he was instantly followed by the burly policeman, who had been on the watch for him. What Patrick Murphy said to the boy Willie never knew, but from that day forward the little interloper was never seen at that street corner any more.

When Father Burton heard of Willie's anxiety about his business he sent for a trustworthy little fellow who attended the Sisters' school, but was not as yet a choir boy. The child gladly promised to take Willie's place for that day, and even refused the payment the kind priest offered him for doing so.

Thus Willie's anxieties were removed and the child was able to join fully in all the joyful anticipation of his comrades.

The day was drawing nearer and nearer and yet no one knew what Father's plans were, for when he was asked, he only answered with a smile that it was all to be a surprise.

At last the morning came, clear and bright, with just a pleasant snap in the air, and long before the ap-

...the coarse-spoken, rough lad who had been annoying Willie for several weeks came and jostled him...

pointed time all the eager boys had assembled around the rectory. To their surprise there were no wagonettes or other vehicles in sight, and Jimmy Windham, a sour-looking boy, who was always dissatisfied about something, began to grumble that he felt sure it was all going to be a take-in and a failure. The Sisters mistrusted this Jimmy very much, for they had several times discovered him, not in mischief—that they expected of boys—but in deceit and underhanded insubordination. They even began to fear they would have to expel him from the school, though they were loath to do so, because he was the only son of a worthy and pious woman who would, they knew, be brokenhearted about the matter.

In spite of Jimmy's grumblings, however, all the other boys were on the tiptoe of expectation, for they all knew they could trust Father Burton not to disappoint them. He soon came out accompanied by two of his assistants and said cheerily:

"All here, boys! That's right! Now we'll start for the depot, for we are going by train to begin with. It is too far to drive this time."

"Hurrah!" shouted the boys enthusiastically.

Just then Willie hurried up anxiously. "Oh, *please,*

Father, couldn't we wait just a few minutes? Herbert isn't here yet!"

Father Burton laughed, for Herbert, though such a good lad in other ways, was noted for being always behind time.

"Late again, is he?" said Father. "Well, I'd be sorry for him to lose his treat, but we can't all miss the train on his account."

"I'll wait for him and bring him on by car if need be," said Father Allison, one of the young priests.

"Well, yes, if you don't mind, but don't wait for him too long. I shall need you over there," answered Father Burton, and they all went off, Willie looking back anxiously every now and then and praying hard that his friend might arrive in time.

The train was in the station and all the boys had taken their seats, yet Father Allison and Herbert had not appeared, and all began to feel quite anxious, for both were great favorites. Father Burton spoke to the conductor and he delayed the train as much as he dared, but he had already given the signal to start when the two appeared, running for all they were worth, and jumped onto the train just as it was moving off.

"We'll leave you behind another time," said Father

Burton, shaking his head at Herbert. "If it had not been for Willie I should have done so today just to give you a lesson, but I knew how it would disappoint your friend."

"Oh, thank you, Father!" said Herbert gratefully. "I'll never be late again."

"Not till next time," laughed Father Burton good-naturedly. "Now, boys," he added, "I'll tell you part of our plan. To begin with, we are going to San José. You know that's a beautiful little place on the coast with lots of rocks and caves, where you can fish and collect seaweeds, shells, and so forth for the Convent museum."

"Oh, grand!" shouted the boys. "May we bathe, sir?"

"Yes, just in one place, where we tell you to, but the rest of the coast is dangerous, so you must not go in without leave. Still, you may put on bathing suits to paddle about among the rocks. We have seen to it that there will be plenty of suits ready for you."

So when they got to their destination the delighted youngsters all rushed to the boathouse and got into bathing suits and then paddled about along the shore and had a good swim in the one safe swimming pool. Then they lay down in the warm sun to rest.

The only one who could not join in all this sport was Willie, but he enjoyed watching the others and looking at the fantastically shaped rocks along the coast and at the beautiful and varied colors of the ocean. Away from the shore the water was deep, deep blue with long stretches of purple where the kelp beds lay. Nearer land and among the rocks it was all manner of tints, from deep red-purple in the shaded coves to almost grass-green where it lay in shallow pools along the rocks. As the morning wore on the breeze increased, and even out at sea the waves were tipped with white, while as they came in-land they swelled into great rollers that broke with a thundering roar on the sands or dashed up in great masses of spray on the rocks.

"The sea is getting too rough for any more swim-ming, boys," called out Father Burton, "but you may play about among the rocks so long as the tide is out."

Jimmy Windham scowled behind the kind priest's back and growled:

"It's a shame to spoil our fun just as the swimming was getting exciting. I know a cove just round the corner. Let's go there," he added to two or three of the worst boys, who always formed his bodyguard.

Just then Herbert and Willie came up.

"Where are you going?" they asked.

"Oh, just a little bit farther, round that headland. It's a fine place for collecting seaweed."

"Is it? We'll go with you, then, for there isn't much here and we promised Sister some fine specimens," said Herbert.

The boys were not too well pleased, for though they thought they could lead Herbert into mischief, they rather feared Willie's straightforward gaze.

"Oh, it will be too rough walking for Willie, but you can come, Herbert," they answered.

"Come where?" said Father Allison, who had just approached.

"Just round to Green Cove to get seaweed, Father," answered Jimmy.

"If it's only to get seaweed, Willie can very well go with you, and mind, boys, you must not attempt to bathe or even to go out among the rocks. Green Cove is noted for its dangerous undertow."

"All right, Father," shouted the boys as they hurried off.

For a few minutes they all pretended to join Herbert and Willie in their search for beautiful specimens, then suddenly Jimmy exclaimed:

"See how calm and peaceful the water is here. It's all nonsense about the undertow. Why shouldn't we go in swimming?"

"Why? Because Father forbade you to," exclaimed Willie.

"Father didn't know how quiet it would be, and besides priests are always over nervous about things. I'm sure this cove is safe. Just look how beautiful the water is."

"Why, yes, it does look lovely!" said Herbert hesitatingly.

"Oh, well! If you're afraid, you needn't come. You're one of the goody-goody kind, who pretend to be good because you're just too much of a coward to dare anything."

"I'm not a coward, I'm not afraid," exclaimed Herbert, who was easily led.

"Well, come along then," said the others as they prepared to go into the water.

"Herbert, you shall not go," said Willie, hurrying forward and resolutely planting himself between his friend and the treacherous waters. "How could you be so disobedient to Father Allison after he took all that trouble to prevent your missing your train, and you a Promoter, too!"

Herbert hung his head shamefacedly while Willie went on hotly.

"And I think it's horrid and ungrateful of all you boys to do what Father has forbidden, when he's taken so much trouble to give us all this treat. If you go in, I'll go and tell him, for I know that cove is dangerous."

"Go, then, you sneaking little hypocrite, go!" shouted Jimmy Windham as he dashed into the water, and three of his friends followed him, but kept fairly near the shore, not feeling any too safe.

Herbert had felt indignant at the way Jimmy had spoken to his friend, and he followed Willie as he hurried up the bluff to join the rest of the party on the other side of the headland.

Just as they had reached the top of the hill and were standing about a stone's throw from the life-saving station, they heard cries for help, and looking back saw Jimmy rolled over and over by a big wave which had just swept in and which carried him out again with it as it receded. One or two of the other boys made futile attempts to get to him, but they, too, were rolled over and, fortunately for them, tossed upon the shore.

"Run, run for Father!" shouted Willie to Herbert.

"I'll go back with this saving line and try to throw it out to Jim."

Just then, fortunately for young Windham, two gentlemen came round on the other side of the cove. Seeing the boy's danger, one of them went out as far as he dared after him, but gave it up in despair and cried, "For God's sake, get a lifeline!"

"Where is it?" shouted the other. Then to his intense relief he saw Willie hurrying down with it and rushed up to meet him.

By the time Father Burton arrived Jimmy had been brought to land, and the other boys, pale and scared, were standing round his apparently lifeless form. He was quickly carried to a neighboring house and such prompt measures were taken to restore him to life that in less than half an hour the doctor who had been called declared him out of danger.

Father Burton had sent Herbert and Willie back to join the rest of the party, with strict injunctions that they should say nothing of their comrade's danger, as he did not wish to cast a gloom on the day which was to have been such a delightful one. He also sent word to Father Allison to hire a yacht and take all the party out for a sail on the bay. They enjoyed it immensely, for the sea was not rough enough to make anyone ill, and the air was fresh and invigorating.

As for the three boys who had gone into the waters of the cove with Jimmy Windham, Father sternly bade them go to the bathhouse and get dressed. When they came out again, very crestfallen and anxious, he took them back to the station and sent them home under the care of the guard, saying he refused to take charge of boys who could not be trusted and who were not only disobedient, but underhanded. He also told them that for the next six months they would be deprived of the privilege of being altar boys and would only be readmitted if they showed by their behavior that they were truly repentant.

When the yachting party came in and Herbert heard of the other boys' punishment, he blushed painfully and exclaimed:

"Oh, Father! if it hadn't been for what Willie said to me, I'd have gone in, too!"

"Well, it's good for you that you listened to Willie's advice," said Father Burton. "It was honest of you to tell me of your temptation, my lad, and I need not punish you, as you did not give way to it. You can't do better than keep wee Willie for your friend always. He's as true as steel, that little chap."

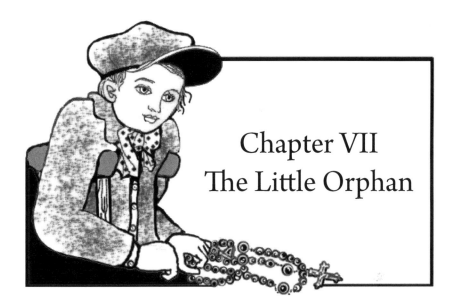

Chapter VII
The Little Orphan

S hortly before noon all the boys went into the boathouse to tidy up a bit, and when they came out, a delightful surprise awaited them. What do you think it was? Why, a whole troop of donkeys were there for them to ride on, and there was also a small trap for the Fathers, who took Willie in with them.

They started inland, and after a fairly long ride, during which time the boys had much merriment over some of the donkeys who would not go, and others who would go too well, they all arrived in high spirits at a pretty ranch nestling on a hill in the pine forest. There they dismounted, and after giving their donkeys in charge of one of the farmhands they went off to a green field, where under the shadow of the great trees the good women of the farm were preparing a plentiful repast.

"Would some of you boys like to come and see us milk the cows while the dinner is cooking?" said the farmer's wife.

"Oh, yes!" a lot of them cried. "That will be great fun." So they followed her into a shed by the side of the pasture, and there she sat down on a low stool and began to milk the first cow.

"It looks very easy to do," said one of the boys.

"Yes," answered the good woman, "but it's like everything else; you must know how to do it right."

"Oh, I know the right way," said one of the boys with an important air. "I learned all about it at my grandfather's."

"Did you ever know anything that Bill White couldn't do?" laughed one of his comrades, for Bill was known to be the greatest boaster in the school.

"Well, I'll show you I can do it," said Bill, "if this lady'll let me."

"Certainly," said the farmer's wife with a smile, as she removed the pail she had been milking into and put another in its place, "but don't try it unless you really know how, else Brown Bess might get cross and kick."

"Oh, I can do it all right!" exclaimed Bill, settling himself on the little low stool and starting as he thought to milk the cow, but no milk came, and his comrades began to laugh derisively.

"Oh, I remember now!" exclaimed Billy, "you have to punch up like," and he suited the action to the word, but Brown Bess evidently disapproved of the proceeding, for in another minute the pail, the boy, and the stool were all rolling on the ground.

"Did she kick you? Are you hurt?" asked the farmer's wife anxiously.

"Oh, no, thank you, ma'am," said Billy ruefully. "It was only the pail knocked me over, but I think she must be a very cross cow. Now at my grandfather's——"

"The cows were differently made, weren't they, Billy?" laughed one of the elder boys, and all the others made such fun of him that Bill strode off indignantly to join another party of boys.

Soon dinner was served, and they all sat down on the grass, all except Willie, who leaned up against a tree. They had new-laid eggs, delicious butter, cream cheese, roast chicken, and all manner of nice fresh vegetables, and finished up with all they could eat of strawberries and cream.

They agreed they'd never tasted a more delicious meal, and I can tell you all did full justice to it, for the morning at the beach and the sail on the bay had given them a hearty appetite.

After dinner was over they were allowed to stroll about the farm and surrounding woods for a time. Then they assembled on a large open field where they had all manner of games, a running race, donkey race, leaping contests, and finally a walking match, which was won by Willie, whose triumph was greeted with much applause. Father Burton gave prizes to all the winners and then they dispersed into the woods again.

All of a sudden one of the boys came rushing back to the Fathers, crying out in terror: "Oh, Father! A bear! A bear is after me!" Just then there was a great scrambling in the underbrush and an old black sow ran by them grunting vigorously and followed by her eight little piggies, squealing for all they were worth. Of course there was a lot of fun over Tommy's bear, and the laughter had hardly subsided when another of the boys, wishing to have a rest, spied what he thought a nice little hillock and sat down on an ants' nest. Of course the ants immediately swarmed out and upon him.

Fortunately for him they were not of a stinging kind, and his comrades did their best to brush them all off him, but he declared he was sure he would feel "*anty*" all over for the rest of the day. His remark was greeted with peals of laughter and he was nicknamed "Auntie" for many a long day after that. While his companions were amusing themselves Willie wandered around to the back of the farm. There found a pale-faced little girl, whose great dark eyes were sad and wistful, and who sat on the back steps of the house sewing.

The little cripple noticed how longingly the child looked at the boys and their games, and going up to her, he began to chat in his pleasant way.

After a time he asked why her mother did not let her have a holiday and join them in their day's fun.

"I've got no mother nor father," said the child sadly. "My parents was Mexicans. I'm an orphan now. I've got nobody what wants me, or wishes to help me, so I was sent out here to the farm, and I've got to work hard to earn the food I eats and the clothes they gives me. They ain't unkind to me, but nobody cares anything about me. I'm just the little drudge what's got to do all the jobs nobody else wants to, and when the rest of the work is done, I has to sew all the time. I never gets no holidays, Sundays, or any other days."

"Why, don't you even go to church!" exclaimed Willie.

"Oh, no! There ain't no church about here—no Catholic church, I mean, and I wouldn't wish to go to no other. I knows Mother wouldn't have liked me to go to any church but my own."

"Oh, are you a Catholic? I'm so glad!" exclaimed Willie, "but I'm ever so sorry for you for not having a mother and not being able to go to church. Why don't you speak to Father Burton? He's ever so kind and perhaps he might be able to help you."

"Oh, I shouldn't dare!" said the child nervously. "I don't know him and the farmers might be angry if they thought I'd complained, you see. They often tells me I'm ungrateful and all that. I sleeps out there over the stables. At nights I'm so frightened I can't sleep, and if I says anything about it they gets cross!"

"I see," said Willie pensively. "I wish I could help you," he added, "and I'll talk to Mother about you. Of course you can always say your prayers, though you can't go to church, and praying helps one a lot and keeps one from feeling lonesome, doesn't it?"

"Yes," said little Antonia rather doubtfully. "But sometimes I think even the good God doesn't care for the likes of me, for I prays and prays for things and He doesn't seem to hear me."

"Oh, you mustn't think that," said Willie earnestly. "Our dear Lord always hears us, Father Burton says, only He doesn't always grant us our prayers at once, because He knows it will be best for us to have to wait and be patient for a while."

So the two children talked on eagerly, Willie encouraging the little girl and giving her renewed hope of a brighter future, and Antonia looking up at her new friend with looks that told of her confidence and gratitude.

"You're ever so kind to talk to the likes of me," she exclaimed. Then she added sadly, "But when you go away and gets back to your nice home you'll forget all about me."

"Indeed I won't," exclaimed Willie. "I never forget any of my friends, and I'll speak about you to Father Burton this very day."

Willie was very eager to do this, and he soon found an opportunity to talk to Father Burton about the poor little girl.

The kind priest was immensely interested, and

found an excuse to stop and talk to the child as if by chance. He afterward questioned the farmer about the little girl and discovered that her story was but too true. The poor child was quite friendless in the world. The farmers, worthy folk as they were, looked upon her with hardly as much interest as upon one of their horses or cattle.

After ascertaining the child's history, Father Burton went back to her and promised to interest himself in her welfare.

So when Willie went to take leave of Antonia he found her much cheered and comforted, and very grateful to her little friend.

But the happy day was passing all too fast and the Fathers had to give the signal for the boys to remount their donkeys and ride back to the shore. Willie again rode with the Fathers, and as they drove away he waved a friendly farewell to little Antonia.

When they arrived at the beach they had a sumptuous supper on the sands, with all manner of cold meats, delicious cakes, and fruits, and then, when the light was beginning to wane, they took the train back home and arrived at San Francisco very tired with their long day's outing. All declared it had been one of the very happiest days in their lives.

As for our Willie, he was all excitement about his little friend Antonia. His joy was boundless when a few weeks later Father Burton told him that he had succeeded in getting her into a Catholic orphanage conducted by Sisters of Mercy, where she was very happy and gave great satisfaction.

Soon after that Antonia sent Willie a letter, very poorly written and peculiar as to spelling, but full of the deepest gratitude toward the little friend who had been the first to sympathize with her.

Chapter VIII
Willie's Revenge

When Willie had spoken of the boy who had been trying for weeks to take his place on the corner, he had, with his characteristic sweetness of disposition, been stating things very mildly.

This boy, a swarthy lad of about thirteen, had been fairly persecuting the little cripple for weeks, in the hope of driving him from his corner. He took every opportunity of rumpling or soiling his papers so as to make them unsaleable, or he would rush between Willie and a customer, or knock and jostle him about whenever he could do so unobserved.

Willie had borne all this with wonderful patience,

but being a nervous, sensitive child, he had suffered very much from the constant strain and worry of it. When the boy, whose name was Richard Smith, suddenly ceased coming to his corner, he felt an intense relief.

His troubles were not over, however, for the lad was all the more angry with Willie for having, as he thought, got him into trouble. He would waylay him as he went to and from his corner and play all the mean tricks he could think of. One wet day, when Willie was hastening home in the pelting rain, he snatched the poor child's waterproof cloak from his shoulders and threw it out into the muddy street, where the little cripple had great trouble in picking it up. He could not get it on again, as he was hampered by a great bundle of papers he was carrying, and he was wet to the skin before he got home, though fortunately he did not catch cold. Another time Richard threw a hard ball at him, which hit him right on the top of the ear and hurt him very much for many days.

"Hullo! Didn't know you were there, little shrimp!" called Dick derisively as he walked away.

Matters had been going along like this for a long time, when one day Willie was going down an almost deserted side street and saw two boys giving a vigorous thrashing to a third smaller one, whom they were holding down and who was yelling vigorously.

"What are you fellows doing there?" cried Willie indignantly. "It's cowardly to hit a fellow when he's down, and two big boys against a smaller one isn't fair."

"What's that to you! Mind your own business," shouted one of the lads. Then looking up he added, "Oh, it's the little cripple fellow! Well, you wouldn't find fault if you knew what we're punishing him for. It's that Dicky Smith. He's been at his tricks again. I guess he's no friend of yours after all he's done to you. Now he shall pay for it, for we've lost our lunch several times, and today we caught him stealing it. He's still got some of it about him. You call the cop, little 'un, while we hold him down."

"Oh, no, don't, don't! I'll never do it again," shrieked the boy, who had a wholesome dread of the policeman.

"Oh, don't give him up to the police," pleaded Willie. "He might go to prison for stealing, and Mother says that when once a fellow is known as a jailbird it wrecks the whole of his life. You've given him a thrashing. Let him go and give him just one more chance. Please, please do!"

"Another chance to rob us of our meal, and cut a hole in our ball, and do all his confounded tricks, not if I know it!" exclaimed the bigger of the boys. "How would you like to go without your dinner yourself?"

"I know it's bad," answered Willie. "But you know if you were afraid of being given up to the police you'd like to have just one more chance. Here! I've got two dimes that are my own. If I give them to you to buy your luncheon, won't you let him go just this once? I'll never beg him off again if he troubles you after this."

"Well, you're a good little chap, I'm sure, after the way he's been bothering you. Now, Smith, will you swear you'll never play any of your tricks on us again?"

"Yes," answered Richard in a surly voice.

"Now mind, we've got our eye on you, so if you get up to your tricks again, sure as you're there we'll give you up to the cop. Hope he won't make you wish you hadn't been so kind to him, little 'un. You're a bully little chap, anyhow!"

So saying, the two big boys went away, leaving Richard and Willie together. The little cripple helped Dick to brush some of the dust off his clothes and then, noticing that his face was bleeding and that he had a black eye, he said gently:

"Here, come home with me. Mother'll be in just now, and she'll put some stuff on your face to prevent it from swelling up."

Still rather surly and shamefaced, Richard followed his little protector, and on the way he growled ungraciously, "I can't think why you stuck up for me like that, for I've been real mean to you often enough."

"Oh, well, you know, Our Lord says we must do good, especially to those who are unkind to us," answered Willie.

"Oh, I see! You're one of the goody-goody kind. Do you believe in all that bosh, really? I don't. My stepfather don't believe in anything neither, says there ain't no such thing as God."

"Oh, how dreadful!" exclaimed Willie. "Then I don't wonder you're—"

"I'm what?" asked Richard angrily.

"Well—not exactly kind, you know," said Willie evasively.

"You mean I'm a good-for-nothing little blackguard," said the other fiercely. "That's what my stepfather calls me."

"Oh, no! I would never say such things," answered

the cripple, "but I thought you'd never been taught to be kind to others, that's all."

Just then they arrived at Mrs. Browne's cottage, and the latter gave an exclamation of dismay at the sight of the disheveled, bleeding, be-mudded boy.

"He's a comrade of mine that's had a bad time, Mother," said Willie. "I thought you'd help him and put some of that good stuff of yours on his face."

"Certainly," said kind Mrs. Browne, and she bathed and cared for the boy's battered face and brushed his clothes, and did not let him go home until he was presentable once more.

"Well, thank you, ma'am, and thank you, Kiddo," said Dick bluntly, as he started to go. "I'm sorry you're one of them awfully good chaps," he added when he was on the sidewalk with Willie, "else we might have been friends. But I never could be friends with a goody-goody kid."

"If I hadn't been one, though, I wouldn't have begged you off just now, would I?" answered Willie with a smile.

"That's true, too," said the other thoughtfully. "Well, I won't forget you did me a good turn, young 'un. If the cop had reported me to my stepfather, he'd have turned me out of the house for sure. He hates me like poison and Mother has trouble enough to get him to let me stay with her. Mother thinks I'm all right, and go to school regular, and everything. Good thing she doesn't know all!"

"You don't mean to say you don't tell your mother everything!" exclaimed Willie.

"Why, of course I don't! Pretty kettle of fish there'd be if she knew. I expect she will know some day, and then—"

"It would be much better to tell her yourself than let her find out from others," said Willie. "Mothers are so kind they always forgive you if you tell them everything yourself, and she'll be sure to hear of it all in time, people always do."

Dick's only answer was a shrug of the shoulders as he went off.

Willie thought he would very likely never hear anything more of the boy. Indeed, he very much hoped he wouldn't, for he instinctively felt that the lad was anything but a desirable acquaintance.

It was almost a year afterward when, to his surprise, he received the following short letter:

DEAR LITTLE KID: I thought over what you said to me that day you helped me out, and I made up my mind to tell mother everything, and you were right—she was ever so kind. She thought I'd better come out here to an uncle in the country. I'm not like you. Don't suppose I'll ever be, but I'm keeping straight, and I guess I owe it to you. I've been saving up my money to buy you something, 'cause I don't forget the two bits. Hope you'll like it.

Your friend,
RICHARD SMITH

The letter, which gave no address, was accompanied with a pretty scarf pin, and Willie's only regret was that he could not write to thank Dick and tell him how happy the letter had made him.

Chapter IX
The Prodigal Son

Willie came round by his mother's chair and caressingly laid his rosy cheek against hers, while he said in a coaxing voice:

"What's troubling you, Mother dear? Are you thinking of Bob?"

"You dear child," answered Mrs. Browne, kissing him tenderly, "how do you always guess my very thoughts? Yes, I was thinking about your brother, grieving about him, wondering what has become of him. I've written and written to that last address in Los Angeles and I can get no answer. Do you know, Willie, if I could have seen him die a holy death like your dear father, I'd sooner know him dead than think of him as I do now."

"Perhaps it's not as bad as you think, Mother dear. Perhaps he's only trying to save up a lot of money and give you a surprise."

Mrs. Browne shook her head.

"That's not like Bob," she said sadly. "He used to be a good-hearted, willing little chap, but he was always one of those happy-go-lucky sort and easily led by anybody he came across."

Willie wound his free arm lovingly round her neck. "Don't grieve, Mother dearest. There's so many of us praying hard for him that I feel sure he'll come back all right before long."

And what had become of this much loved son all this time? He was very skillful in his trade as an electric operator, and at first he had obtained a first-class situation, as he had told his mother. But he had met with very undesirable companions in the city and they dragged him down until he became a drunkard and gambler like themselves. Not only did he give up all his religious duties, not only did he spend all his money on pleasure, but he got himself dismissed from every decent situation because he could not keep sober, and at last he found himself penniless, homeless, and without prospect of getting work. Then he thought of his mother, not as the prodigal son remembered his father, with shame and contrition and desire to make amends, but simply as one who would be sure to help him as far as she could.

He had a rather handsome watch and chain which he had bought when he first came to the city, and he sold that in order to get the money for his journey. On his way he had been busy making up a story of having been out of work through hard times, the jealousy of others, and so forth, and he quite chuckled to himself when he thought how easy it would thus be to deceive that loving mother and make himself out as having had a brave struggle against difficulties.

At last he was back in his native town. How familiar everything looked—it made him think of old times when he had been a bright and happy boy there. Ah! that was the well-known street corner where he had so often stood to take the car to go to work, and there—surely that never could be wee Willie, the little crippled brother he used to be so fond of?

"Hullo, Kiddo!" he exclaimed, "what are you doing here?"

It was over two years since Willie had seen his

brother, yet in spite of the change in his appearance he recognized him in a minute and unconsciously a feeling of shame came over him as he gazed at the ill-dressed, sallow-complexioned, dissipated-looking young workman. They certainly presented a strange contrast.

The child looked his brother squarely in the face with those honest, fearless eyes of his and answered:

"I'm working for Mother and the girls. We've found it hard to get on at times, while you've been away. Nancy nearly went blind, but she's wonderfully better now. Poor Mother'll be glad to see you, for she has fretted for you so much. At times it was all I could do to comfort her. But we've prayed for you so hard that I felt sure you'd come back all right."

Robert felt as if rooted to the spot and unable to utter a word, so crushed did he feel by the surging emotions that his little brother's words and the look of that pure, sweet face, had brought into his heart.

While he, the big, strong, eldest brother, who ought to have been the mainstay of the family, had been giving himself up to pleasure and self-indulgence, this brave little sufferer had, in spite of his infirmity, been helping mother and the girls. This poor wee mite, who was little more than a baby! And had he, Bob, come to bring disgrace and misery to that brave heart? No, he'd die sooner than do that.

"Are you feeling sick? Do you want me to see you home? It's rather a busy time for me, but still——"

"Oh, no, Kiddo, I'll be all right," said Bob, pulling himself together again. "Still at the same place, hey?"

"Yes, and I think Mother'll just about be home. I've got nearly another hour to do yet," said Willie, flying from one customer to another.

On his way home Bob had to pass the church, and he thought he'd go in for a few minutes to get over his emotion. At the sight of the dear, familiar altar a great feeling of rest and peace stole over him in the solitude and silence of the great church, and he fell on his knees with that cry from the heart which Our Lord never rejects.

"God, be merciful to me a sinner!"

When he rose again it was with a firm resolve to tell his mother the whole truth and to live henceforth a different life.

Need I tell of the joy of the poor mother at the return of the prodigal? Need I say how ready she was to forgive him and help him to right himself? No one, she said, need know a word about his past life except Father Burton, and Willie, she was sure, would be able to help him to obtain a situation, for he was such a wonderful little fellow for getting one out of difficulties, and he had so many influential friends.

The very next day Robert went to have a long interview with Father Burton, whose altar boy he had been while quite a little chap. When he came home he had not only received absolution for those two sad years of folly, but he had signed the pledge and sworn to keep it faithfully.

It was not easy at first, but a look at brave little Willie battling against such terrible odds with cheery courage would give his elder brother a fresh incentive to struggle against himself.

As soon as Robert was a little rested and his mother and sister had set his wardrobe in order and made him presentable once more, Willie took him to see what he proudly called, "My friend, the great Dr. Ferris." The child was to introduce his brother and then go on to his work, for Robert had things he wished to tell the doctor which he did not wish the little fellow to know.

"Dr. Ferris—my brother, Robert Browne, whom we call Bob," said Willie in his old-fashioned way, and the doctor smiled as he held out his hand and said kindly:

"I've heard often about this brother Bob, and I'm glad to meet him. If he's in any way worthy of being the brother of my little friend, wee Willie, I shall be more than glad to help him in any way I can."

Bob blushed rather painfully and Willie skipped away to his work with a cheery "Thank you, sir, and good morning, for I must hurry off."

His mother had said that nobody need know anything about her son's past, but the boy felt that it would be dishonorable to expect the doctor to help and recommend him without telling him something of the truth. So in a few words he told him the real facts of the case, then he added:

"I meant to make a bluff about it all to the folks when I got home, but when I saw that dear little crippled chap working so bravely to help Mother and the girls, all of a sudden it came over me what a brute I'd been."

"I quite understand it," answered the doctor, "he made the same impression on me." Then seeing the astonished look on the young man's face, he added, "I don't mean that I have been offending at all in the same way as you have. We have unfortunately many ways of failing in our duty toward God, and to me, as to you, that brave child has been a little apostle by his example. I'm glad you've been so frank and open with me, my lad, for I guessed much of your story the minute I saw you. We doctors are very keen sighted in many ways, you know. Now, electricity isn't much in my line, of course, but I know people who will, I think, be able and willing to help you on my recommendation, and I'll do my best for you, for Willie's sake. Remember this, though, I expect you to be worthy of your brother. I won't say more."

The doctor was as good as his word, and before the week was out Bob was in a good situation in one of the best electric firms of the city, where he had every chance of making a good start in life once more. He proved worthy of the trust that had been put in his promises.

Chapter X
A Surprise Party

As we have already seen, Willie was a dear, sweet, lovable little fellow, and a zealous little Catholic. But he was not perfect, any more than the rest of us, and just now there came upon him one of the bitterest temptations he'd ever had in his short life.

For the last two years or more he had grown to be, as it were, the head of the family, his mother's little confidant and helper, his sister's kindest friend, and the cherished playmate of the little ones. Everyone had seemed to turn to him for everything, and unconsciously he had grown to expect a great deal of love and attention. In fact, he was getting a little con-

At first he had honestly tried to be glad of his brother's return and of his mother's joy, but after a time he was dismayed to find that he was sore and jealous --- yes, jealous!

ceited.

Now that Bob had returned, however, everything seemed changed. His mother, overjoyed to have her eldest back again, seemed entirely wrapped up in him. Nancy was delighted to have an elder brother to go out with, and thought him no end amusing and clever. The little ones found it great fun to romp with him and occasionally be taken for rides on his bicycle. And so our poor Willie found himself rather set aside, and he felt it keenly.

At first he had honestly tried to be glad of his brother's return and of his mother's joy, but after a time he was dismayed to find that he was sore and jealous—yes, jealous! Why should they make so much of Bob, who had left them all to struggle for two whole years, while he, little Willie, had worked so hard for them in spite of his aching leg? Now everything was for Bob, everybody thought only of Bob, even Mother didn't seem like Mother since Bob returned. And then the child, after brooding over all his troubles, would have violent fits of remorse for his jealousy, and altogether he had such a hard struggle with himself that he seemed to lose his ever-ready smile, and there came a sad wistfulness in those brown eyes.

His mother was so busy and so taken up with her thankfulness about Bob and her anxiety that he should keep on the straight road in future that she did not notice the little lad's trouble. From the first, Father Burton had been the confidant of the child's struggle, and Dr. Ferris had also found out the secret of his little friend's changed looks.

Both felt that it was a shame Willie should have cause to feel himself thus slighted, and the first time Father Burton had an opportunity of doing so he told Mrs. Browne what he thought about it. "Killing the fatted calf is all very well," he said hotly, "but there's no reason why Robert, after all his bad behavior, should be made a lion and an idol, and that brave little chap, who has done so much to help you all, should feel himself put aside and forgotten."

"Has Willie been complaining?" asked Mrs. Browne in a vexed voice.

"Willie! Complaining? Is that like him? But I have eyes in my head, and besides, everybody is noticing the little fellow's changed looks—everybody, apparently, but yourself. Go home, Mrs. Browne, and think over the matter, and you will find I'm right in what I say. It's been very natural and wholly unintentional, I'm sure. Still, it shouldn't last."

That evening Bob was out with a friend and Nancy was putting the little ones to bed, while their mother sat in the parlor feeling sad and worried. How was it she had not noticed that there was something the matter with Willie? What sort of a mother could she be to be so blind and careless, she thought.

As she sat thus, reproaching herself, the little fellow came in, and noticing her troubled look, instantly hurried up and said, as he had so often done before:

"What is it, Mother dear? Is something worrying you?"

"Oh, nothing, Willie dear," she said evasively.

"Ah! I used to be your little friend once, and in those days you would always tell me your troubles, but now—" he was going to add, "you have Bob," but checked himself abruptly, while two great tears rolled down his cheeks.

"Oh, Willie! My Willie! That's just what I was troubling about," said his mother, throwing her arms around him and bursting into tears. "You are my little friend still. You always will be my very dearest little friend. You must not think that because I am so happy to have your brother back that I love you any the less, my treasure. You don't know what it was like for me to think that I had lost him, that he was perhaps not doing right! And then when he came back I'm afraid I was selfish in my joy—"

"Oh, Mother, don't, don't!" exclaimed Willie. "It is I who have been so naughty and so jealous. I struggled so hard against it, and I thought you hadn't seen it, Mother, but I'm ever so sorry, and indeed I'll try to be a better boy. I can't bear to think I grieved you, Mother."

"It wasn't your fault, dearest. It was all just a mistake, that's all, but whatever happens, never, never think that anything can alter my love for you!"

And so the two comforted each other, and Mrs. Browne was careful in future that Willie should have no cause to feel slighted.

A few days later Dr. Ferris met Nancy carrying a number of small parcels and looking very pleased and excited.

"What's up, Nancy? Killing the fatted calf still?"

"Oh, no, sir, we've done enough of that long ago," laughed Nancy. "It's for Willie. We're afraid he's been feeling rather left out in the cold lately, because of our excitement over Bob's return."

"I'm glad you feel that way about it at last, Nancy. I was beginning to wonder when you would notice it and where your sense of appreciation and gratitude was located."

"Oh, sir, did *you* notice it? You know we never meant it one little bit, but we were so overjoyed. Now we want to make it up to Willie. It's going to be his birthday tomorrow, and Bob proposed we should get up a grand surprise tea-party for him. He might feel hurt if we said nothing and gave him nothing in the morning, and we couldn't have a surprise party if we told him about it beforehand, so we made up our minds to give it to him today instead."

"I'm very glad. Who are to be the guests?"

"Oh, just ourselves and Father Burton."

"I suppose I couldn't get an invitation," laughed the doctor.

"Oh, sir, we'd love to have you, and Willie'd be so delighted! But we would never dare to invite you."

"You wouldn't! Well, then, I'll invite myself, but don't wait for me, because I may come in rather late."

Nancy flushed with pleasure.

"Oh, that is too kind of you, sir! We will all feel so proud to have you."

"All right, you can reckon on me, but as I said before, don't wait tea for me." Then, as Nancy was going, he called after her: "You don't know of anything

Willie would really like?"

"Yes, sir," said Nancy, running back, "but it's such a big and expensive thing we couldn't get it this time even by joining together."

"What is it?"

"Why, a graphophone, sir. The poor little chap is so fond of music, and he has always longed to have a graphophone to play tunes to him while he lies down."

"Fine!" cried the doctor, who recollected with pleasure that he'd taken a fairly good one in payment for a bad debt and had it stowed away somewhere in the garret.

That evening Willie came home to find a great air of mystery and gaiety in the house, and was much surprised at Nancy's asking him to go up into his own room through the kitchen and make himself tidy.

When he came down to the parlor he found all the family assembled in their Sunday best, and with them dear old Father Burton, and he noticed that the room and the table were all decked with flowers and that at his usual place—one couldn't call it a seat, as he had to stand—was a whole pile of little parcels, nicely arranged and decorated.

"Hurrah for our Willie! A happy birthday to our Willie!" they all cried, and Willie was so touched and so happy he didn't know whether to laugh or to cry. First they all crowded round him and kissed him and said all kinds of loving things to him. Then Bob insisted he should look at his presents, and Mother and Nancy helped him to unpack them one after another. There was a pretty pair of rosary beads from Sister Superior and a pretty holy picture from each of the other Sisters, and a beautiful prayer-book from Father Burton. From Mother there was a lovely book he'd long wanted and two fine new ties from "your grateful brother Bob," and a splendid pair of embroidered suspenders from Nancy, also a pretty notebook from little Polly, and a box of candy from Baby—and oh, another box of homemade fudge from Nancy!

Willie was fairly bewildered with delight.

"I never had such a lovely birthday before!" he exclaimed.

"It was Bob who thought of getting it all up and made the decorations and got the flowers and the—"

"Hush, Mother, hush!" cried Nancy, laughing, "you mustn't tell secrets."

"What! Is there something more?" asked Willie, whose heart was reproaching him bitterly for the jealous thoughts he had entertained about this kind brother Bob.

"Yes, there are two more surprises!" exclaimed Nancy. "Shall we wait to have them together or shall we have them—" but Bob clapped his hand over her mouth with a shout of laughter.

"Let's wait and have them together," he said, and they all settled round the table, where there remained one vacant chair, the second seat of honor beside Willie.

"Who's that for?" he asked.

"Ah, that's one of the surprises," said Mother with a smile, and they began tea as soon as Father Burton had said grace, but all listened anxiously for the expected visitor.

Very soon they heard an auto stop in the street and a quick, businesslike footstep coming up to the door. Nancy ran to open the door.

"Dr. Ferris!" exclaimed Willie, clapping his hands with joy. "Oh, I *am* glad, it is kind of you!" and the brown eyes swam with tears of pleasure.

"A happy, happy birthday to my little friend Willie," cried the doctor, "and I hope you'll enjoy my present and it will often make you think of me."

Willie was so wild with joy he didn't know what to

do. All of a sudden he stopped, after excitedly hopping all about the room on his crutches, and clasping his hands, he exclaimed:

"Isn't God good to give me such a sweet mother and such a dear brother and sisters, and such kind friends! I don't know how to thank Him enough. I don't deserve it," he added, almost sadly. Then he cried with his winning smile, "But oh! I thank you all ever, ever so much, and if I haven't deserved it before, I'll try to deserve it now."

And then they all cheered him, and soon Bob came in, carrying a beautiful iced cake with Willie's name and the date written on it and around it nine little candles of different colors.

"Only nine!" exclaimed the doctor. "I thought my friend Willie had been nine ever since I first met him."

"Oh, no, sir, I said 'getting on for nine,' answered Willie.

"I see, and now you're getting on for ten, I suppose," laughed his friend.

And then they all started tea over again and ate slices of the cake, and laughed and talked, and Dr. Ferris was as simple and friendly as if he'd been in his own home, so that they didn't feel the least bit shy with him.

After tea they set the graphophone going, and Father Burton and the doctor told some amusing stories, and then they all played games. In the middle of it all there was a knock at the door, and who should it be but kind Pat Murphy with a great big box of candy as his birthday present. Altogether, when it was all over and Willie was lying in bed, he thought he'd never had such a delightful birthday or such a happy evening in his life.

"Now, you did not feel yourself forsaken tonight, did you, darling?" said his mother as she came to kiss him good-night.

"Oh, no, indeed, Mother dearest, I feel so sorry, so ashamed for having been so wicked about dear Bob! Do you think God will forgive me?"

"I am sure He has forgiven you already, dearest."

"Do you think Bob would come and kiss me good-night?"

"Certainly, but I don't want you to say anything to him about what you felt."

"All right, Mother, but I'd like to thank him."

And as Willie thanked him effusively, Bob kissed the little fellow and said in a husky voice:

"All right, little Kiddy, I'm ever so glad you enjoyed

it. I never in the world can do half enough to repay you for what you've done for me."

Willie wondered what he could mean, and thought he must be alluding to his having introduced him to Dr. Ferris, which was such a simple thing! That was the end of our little lad's jealousy, first because he never had any further cause for any, and secondly because he had grown so fond of his brother that he never thought anyone could make too much of him.

Chapter XI
Baby's Day with Buddy

O ne day when Willie got home he saw that Nancy was looking very sober and that her eyes were suspiciously red. He looked around from Mother to Nancy, but was afraid to ask questions in case his sister might have been getting into disgrace over something.

Mrs. Browne was the first to speak.

"Nancy is very much disappointed," she said, "because the Sisters have invited her as a member of the Alumni to join them in the great outing they give once a year, and I can't let her go on account of Baby."

"Couldn't Baby go too?" asked Willie.

"No, dear, the Sisters can't take charge of such small children. It is quite enough they should take Polly, and I'm so rushed with work this week that I couldn't possibly stay at home to look after little Muriel."

"Couldn't I look after Baby?" asked Willie. "I often help Nancy take care of the little ones, and it seems a shame I should have had my treat and Nancy shouldn't have hers."

Mrs. Browne hesitated. "I don't see how you could mind Baby and sell your papers, dear," she said anxiously.

"Well, you know I don't sell papers all day, Mother," he said eagerly, "and just for the short time I sell them Muriel might sit by me and she'd be good, wouldn't you, Baby?"

"Oh, yes!" exclaimed the child, clapping her hands. "Baby'll sell papers! Baby'll be welly, welly dood with Buddy! Baby lub Buddy!"

"I'm sure I hardly know what to say," murmured the mother. "I just hate to disappoint Nancy, who doesn't get many treats, and yet it seems too much to put on you, Willie, and you'd have to get a meal for the two of you, and——"

"Oh, Mother! I could prepare the meals in advance," exclaimed Nancy eagerly.

"I feel sure I could manage, Mother," said Willie, "won't you trust me?"

So after much talk and discussion it was agreed that Nancy should go for her treat, and that on his return from selling his morning papers Willie should take possession of Baby, and mind her till his mother came home at six o'clock.

Nancy was most grateful to her brother, because the trip up the mountain was one she had always longed for. On the appointed morning she went off in high glee, looking very pretty in her clean white frock and shady straw hat trimmed with roses, while little Polly danced along by her sister.

Nancy had been up almost before daybreak and had finished preparing a cold luncheon for Willie and Baby and also a dinner, which would only need heating up.

Mrs. Browne stayed from her work an hour later than usual, and as soon as Willie returned she hurried off after having made the baby promise to be very good and not give any trouble to her brother.

Willie was in high spirits and did not feel at all anxious at the thought of what he had undertaken.

To begin with, he put on Baby's crawlers and told her she might play in the backyard and pull up the weeds while he prepared his lessons for the next day. He leaned against a corner of the veranda, from which he could see the little mite.

At first he watched her pretty closely, but she seemed so busy and so good that he became less attentive and was soon deeply engrossed in his history lesson.

Suddenly looking up, he gave a cry of horror and rushed down to the garden, where Baby was busily pulling up, not the weeds, but their mother's choicest annuals, of which she had quite a bunch in her hands.

"Oh, no, Baby!" he cried. "I told you not to touch anything but the weeds in the path."

"I was only picking pitty fowers to make you a surprise," exclaimed poor Baby, bursting into tears and rubbing her face with her muddy hands.

Willie felt touched. "Poor Baby!" he exclaimed. "It was all my fault for not watching you! You didn't mean to be naughty, did you? Don't cry," he added, kissing her and wiping the dirty streaks off her face. Then he set to work carefully replanting the poor flowers, which was a hard task, as stooping was so difficult for him. After he had sprinkled the plants and covered them over to give them a chance to recover, he thought it was too hot for Baby to remain in the garden and took her indoors, where he made her sit on the carpet and play with her toys. At first she was very good, but she got tired of one thing after another and began throwing her Noah's Ark animals all about the room and hammering the floor with her doll's head, which was used to such things, it is true, and had little shape or comeliness to be knocked out of it.

Willie quietly insisted on her getting up and looking for the small wooden animals, and while she was occupied doing this he read another half page of his lesson. Again looking up, he saw Baby calmly sucking the crimson paint off a very angular pig!

Horrified lest she should have poisoned herself, he made her spit vigorously, washed out her mouth and gave her some milk to drink. A little reassured by all these measures, he sat her at the table with a pencil and paper, both of which he thought were harmless things with which the little one could do no mischief.

All went well for a time, and Willie was beginning to congratulate himself on his bright idea, when

one of his mother's customers came to ask for some
shirts which she had left to be laundered. Willie
knew where to find them, and putting his book on
the table, he called out to Baby to sit still and be very
good until he came back. He was some little time
gone, as he had to find paper and wrap up the laun-
dry work before giving it to the customer. When he
returned to the parlor he found that in his absence
Baby had taken possession of his book, and holding
the pencil in her chubby hand as if it were a dagger,
was busily digging into it circles, zigzags, and lines of
all sorts. Poor Willie felt terribly annoyed, for he was
very careful about his books and he saw at a glance
that all this could never be erased. His reproaches
caused another flood of tears, and when they had
both calmed down the boy thought it was time for
their midday meal, and hoped it would prove a wel-
come diversion.

So he set the table, helped little sister up into her
high-chair and they began to eat quite cheerfully.
Willie told the baby a fairy story while they were at
table and she was as good as gold until the end of the
meal, when he gave her some bread and jam and she
wanted more, and more, and more!

Knowing that his mother never allowed her to

have so much, he exclaimed:

"Wait a minute, Baby. I'll go to the pantry and get you an apple."

"Don't want apple, want nice jam," cried willful Baby.

"Oh, but it's such a lovely rosy apple I know you'll like it, and I'll finish telling you the story about the big giant. Sit quietly there till I come back," he added, hurrying out after having put the jam safely on a shelf out of her reach, as he thought.

He was just about to get the apple when he heard a loud crash and fearful screams from Baby, and hurrying back, he found her on the ground with the broken pot of jam, spilling all its contents on the kitchen floor.

Hastily helping his little sister up, he ascertained to his relief that she had only fallen from a low stool on which she had been standing, and was no worse for the tumble except for a bump on her head. This, however, was beginning to swell up, so Willie hastened to fetch a dark-colored salve which his mother kept for such cases and which was very efficacious. He rubbed a little of it on the bump and tried to soothe the naughty little girl, though he scolded her at the same time for being so disobedient and greedy.

"Me want apple, me want apple," roared Baby, and finally Willie went off in search of the apple. He did not seem to have been away long, but while he had been gone the baby had made the most of her time by plastering her hair all over the front with lumps of salve, and a more ridiculous object than she looked could not be imagined. Even poor, harassed, wearied-out Willie could not help bursting into a peal of laughter at her appearance, but afterward he had infinite trouble rubbing off as much as he could of the grease out of her hair. Instead of waving over her forehead in pretty curls, it now stood up like horns about her head.

When he had done his best to repair this last disaster Willie remembered with deep thankfulness that the baby was always put to bed for a couple of hours after dinner, and by the time he had settled her down and repaired some of the damage she had caused, he fairly mopped the perspiration off his face, he was so hot and exhausted.

Fortunately, Baby took her accustomed nap, for she was tired out too. When she woke up again she was in a less restless mood and played about quietly till it was time for her to be dressed and go with Willie to sell his evening papers.

With considerable trouble he got her ready, tied on her bonnet, and felt quite proud of the look of his little sister in her clean frock. He now took her downstairs and told her to wait for him while he shut the back of the house. Unfortunately, there was a pail of soapsuds in the kitchen which his mother had left there that morning, and just as Willie was coming for her, Baby stepped back against it and fell sitting in the soapsuds!

Poor Willie laughed at first, but afterward he could have cried with vexation, for the child's clothes were soaked, and he knew it would be a difficult matter for him to change them for her. He hurried to one of their neighbors, for whom he often ran errands, and she very willingly came to his help and soon changed the little one's clothes and got her ready to start with her brother.

For a time all went well, as the child was delighted with the novelty of standing in the street handing papers to gentlemen and taking pennies for Willie, but after about an hour of it she began to get restless, fretful, and constantly wanting attention. Her bonnet always seemed to be falling off, or her shoestring coming untied, or she got under people's feet, or dropped a paper in the gutter, or a nickel down a drain-hole until poor Willie felt almost crazed. Then a little white dog came around, and she would play with it and pulled it about until it growled, and her brother was in terror lest it should bite her. He tried to drive the dog away, but it kept coming back, and Baby pursued it up and down the pavement, to the annoyance of the passersby.

Finally the dog disappeared for a while, and peace seemed to be restored, for Willie had settled his sister on an empty box and given her a picture paper to look at. It was just his busiest time, and he was very much occupied selling papers when all of a sudden Baby cried, "There my 'ittle wite doggie!" Before anyone could stop her she had darted across the street after him, and slipping on the greasy asphalt, fell but a few yards in front of a heavy street car that was coming round the corner.

Everyone gave a cry of horror, expecting to see the small mite crushed to death, when, in spite of his lameness, Willie darted out like a flash into the road and snatched his sister from between the rails, dragging her into safety just in time. A shout of applause greeted him, but the terrible fright, following on his trying day, was too much for poor little Willie, and when he got back on to the sidewalk he fainted.

*It was his busiest time, and he was
occupied selling his papers...*

When he came to himself, he found a crowd around him and Baby crying and screaming.

He was led into a drugstore opposite, and after restoratives had been given him, he pulled himself together again and insisted on going back to finish selling his papers. Fortunately for him, a kind, motherly neighbor of theirs had seen the accident, and she offered to take Baby home with her till Willie had finished his work. I need hardly say with what relief and gratitude he accepted her offer.

When he got home he found his mother there before him and quite aware of all that had happened, for her neighbor had told her of the children's narrow escape, and Baby had confessed to the greater part of her other misdeeds.

"My poor dear boy!" cried Mrs. Browne, throwing her arms around the little fellow. "What a time you have had with Baby. I don't wonder you look so pale and worn out. Oh! thank God, neither of you children were hurt! When I think of what might have happened!" she added, with tears in her eyes.

"Oh, don't cry, Mother dear! You see it is all right now. I thought I could take better care of Baby, but somehow, every time I was doing something else, she seemed to get into mischief."

"Mother is very displeased with her," said Mrs. Browne, looking severely at her little girl, "and she shall not have the beautiful new doll I had bought for her, thinking she would deserve it as a reward for being good. I shall take it back to the store and buy brother Willie a new book with the money I gave for it."

"Oh, Mamma, forgive me, pease, pease! I'll never be naughty any more. Buddy, ask Mamma to forgive Baby!" sobbed the child.

"Please, Mother, forgive her," pleaded Willie, "for my sake, Mother dear," he added coaxingly, as his mother shook her head.

"No, Willie dear," she said firmly. "It is just like you to wish her to be forgiven, but indeed, dear, it would be a mistaken kindness to your little sister. Today she was greedy, she tried to steal what she had been forbidden to have, and she was terribly disobedient. The doll shall go back, and if it were not that brother Willie has asked me to forgive you, Baby, I'd give you a good spanking in the bargain."

They all had had supper and Baby had been put to bed before Nancy and Polly came in, very tired and sleepy, but brimming over with joyful accounts of the perfectly lovely time they'd had.

Nancy looked distressed when she heard of all Willie's troubles and tribulations.

"Poor brother!" she exclaimed, "you must have wished you hadn't let me go."

"Oh, no, I never wished that," answered Willie. "I only wish I was a better hand at taking care of babies. I thought you must need a holiday badly after having Baby to mind every day for so long! I'm ever so glad you had such a lovely time, Sis."

"Yes, I had a perfectly splendid day, and I owe it all to you, as I do so many things," said Nancy, as she put her arm round her little brother and gave him a good hug.

Chapter XII
The Two Portraits

It was strange how everybody seemed to find it quite natural to confide their sorrows to Willie, not that he was by any means an inquisitive child, but I suppose it was on account of his sympathetic nature and perfect reticence.

Dr. Ferris, for instance, though kindly and affable, was a very reserved man and had come to San Francisco in order to avoid the indiscreet condolences of his friends and acquaintances. One morning, however, the child had run in to see if he could do any errand for him, and had found him sitting at his desk looking sadder than usual. Half unconsciously, the little lad came up to his friend, and laying his hand caressingly on his arm, murmured, "I'm so sorry you feel unhappy."

"How do you know I feel unhappy? You must be a mind reader," said the doctor, with a smile, as he patted the boy's curly head.

"A mind reader! Oh, I hope not. Isn't that something rather wicked? No, I can see it in your face. I've seen Mother look like that often when Bob was away."

"Yes, your happy mother! She's got her boy safely home again," said the doctor with a sigh.

"Yes, you see we all prayed so hard."

"So have I, but I don't seem to get my prayer granted. Won't you pray for me, Willie?"

"Oh! I do! Lots, and so does Nancy. Every day, every day, we pray hard, both of us, but I tell you what," said the child, looking up at the doctor with his beaming smile, "I've thought of something. Do you know, Father Burton says I may make my First Holy Communion next month. Isn't it lovely? I've been longing and longing for it! And Sister says that one's sure to have anything granted that one prays for earnestly on that day, and I'll make that my intention."

"You dear child!" exclaimed the doctor with a tremor in his voice, "then I can indeed hope on. Do you know that I had a dear little boy who would now be about your age?"

"Yes, I heard it," said the child.

"You heard it! Well, someone who ought to be very dear to me took him away and I've never been able to find him since."

"I know! I'm so sorry for you," said Willie, his brown eyes filling with tears.

"Shall I show you the portrait of my little lad as I saw him last?" said the doctor, pulling out of his pocket a worn leather case in which were two portraits, one of a beautiful, stylishly dressed young woman, the other of a lovely boy of six, with great dark eyes, curly hair, and a winning, intelligent expression.

"Isn't he dear!" said Willie. "What was his name?"

"Arthur. But God only knows where he is. I've had him searched for the world over. Well, now remember I reckon on your prayers to find him, Willie," added the doctor as there came a knock at the door and a patient was announced.

For the next month Willie was busier than ever, for although he did not give up his papers or his studies, he spent much time preparing for his First Holy Communion, about which he was intensely in earnest.

He little knew how much quiet work for God he did there at his street corner, how many people discouraged, dissatisfied, tired of the struggle against difficulties, felt ashamed at the sight of the brave little cripple's constant cheeriness and encouraged by it to try again and do better themselves.

"Isn't that child an inspiration!" exclaimed a hard working woman as she looked back at him one day. "When I think life's hard, I've only got to come and look at him, and it does me more good than a long sermon on patience."

At last the longed-for day was fast approaching and the whole family was busy making preparations. It wasn't that Mrs. Browne meant to turn it into a day of festivities which might distract the dear child, but she had thought it would be kind to invite two old country cousins who were childless themselves and lived a rather lonely life on a farm far out in the country.

The day before the First Holy Communion the old people arrived, and very odd and countrified they seemed, and quite dazed in the hurry and bustle of a

*When the great day came, and Willie went up to the altar
and received his dear Lord for the first time,
his happiness knew no bounds.*

big town, but delighted with the pleasant change and much flattered at having been thought of and invited.

When the great day came, and Willie went up to the altar and received his dear Lord for the first time, his happiness knew no bounds. Those who loved him felt their hearts filled with thankfulness as they watched his rapt expression and deep earnestness.

To his great joy, not only his mother, Bob, and Nancy followed him to the communion rail, but also Dr. Ferris and even Patrick Murphy, who had long since joined the League of the Sacred Heart, and persuaded several others to do so. Both he and the doctor had to hurry off as soon as Mass was over, but before doing so the latter had slipped into Willie's hand a tiny box to be opened when he got home. And what do you think it contained? A watch! A real silver watch with his initials and the date engraved inside the case.

"Oh, Mother!" said Willie, as he threw himself into his mother's arms on his return home, "I'm too happy! I feel as if my heart would burst with happiness!" He did not mention how terribly his leg and back were aching from his long standing and brave attempt to kneel on one leg.

Chapter XIII
A Holiday in the Country

The old country cousins were so delighted with the kind reception they had received and so charmed with their cousin's children, especially Willie and the little ones, that nothing would satisfy them but that they must take some of them back to the farm for a holiday. Willie had been working so hard that he was looking rather pale and wan, and they thought the fresh country air and complete change would do him a world of good, and all his friends thought so, too.

The child longed to go, for the idea of staying at a farm charmed him above everything, but he was afraid of losing his corner and his regular customers.

It was only after the other boys had promised no one should be allowed to take his place, and Patrick Murphy had assured him that he'd give an eye to this being enforced, that Willie consented to go for a whole week, which seemed to him quite a long time to be away from "my business," as he called it.

The old people would not hear of allowing the other child, Polly, to come home so soon, and as the farm was far from the railway and very difficult of access, Dr. Ferris very kindly said that he needed an outing, too, and that at the end of the week he would drive over in his auto and fetch the little lad home.

The two children were wild with joy as they started off with the old country folk. The railway journey they found rather tedious, but when they got out at a little country station and found a regular farm wagon with a good strong dappled gray horse waiting for them, it was quite a novel and exciting experience. To be sure, Willie had some trouble in scrambling up, for the step seemed about half a mile high and the horse was restless, but when they were all safely packed in, bag and baggage, and old Cousin Sam whipped up the gray horse, it was simply grand! The green fields with large herds of cattle lazily browsing, the orchards laden with fruit, the dark pine forests all around, everything filled the city children with wonder and delight.

Then when they got to the farm, how quaint and novel the old house seemed, with its great rambling kitchen, its old-fashioned parlor with chintz-covered furniture and artificial flowers under a glass and its old pictures of the time of the Civil War.

Then the next morning what a delightful experience to be awakened by the sounds of the busy farmyard and to go out after breakfast and help the old folk milk the cows, and churn the butter, and gather the eggs in the poultry yard. All the animals on the farm were pets to the old people, who had never had any children to lavish their love upon. On hot afternoons, when it was almost too sunny to play about comfortably, Cousin Sam would take the youngsters out some little distance to a quiet stream rippling and gurgling over its stony bed in a cool canyon. There they would stay and fish, or Polly would take off her stockings and paddle in the water while Cousin Sam taught Willie how to make whistles from the reeds.

Every day, when they went to the stream, they passed by a tiny cottage, so deeply embedded in flowering vines as to be almost hidden from the road. The second day Polly asked if anybody lived there or if it were "a shut-up house."

"Well, it is a very shut-up house, as you call it," said the old man, "but a widow lady lives in it with her little boy. She is very haughty and stand-offish, and although she's been there coming on two years, she's made no acquaintances. If she weren't so haughty like, I'd take yer there, for that pore little kid must be powerful lonesome."

Willie's eyes opened wide with astonishment and interest.

"Are you sure she's a widow? How old is the little boy?" he asked eagerly.

"The little 'un? 'Bout your age, a handsome little chappie, too, with big black eyes."

"Don't you think the lady would let us play with her little boy?" asked Willie.

"No, I don't for a minute think she'd so much as let yer speak to him," said his cousin conclusively, and Willie had to rest satisfied for that day.

The next afternoon the old man was tired out with his hot morning's work and he sent the children down to the brook together. As they passed by the cottage a curtain was pulled back and a pair of longing eyes looked after the two children, who seemed so happy and were chatting so merrily together,

Polly carrying the fishing tackle and pail, and Willie's crutches beating time quickly on the hard road.

At first all went well enough, and they did not miss Cousin Sam so very much, but all of a sudden Polly stepped out too far onto a wet, slippery stone, and with a cry of terror fell splash into the water. The brook was not deep just there, and by steadying himself on his crutches, Willie was able to drag his little sister to land, but she was wet and frightened, and her piercing screams made the very woods ring.

Poor Willie felt terribly puzzled about what to do, and was vainly trying to quiet the child when a lady suddenly appeared from behind some trees and asked in a gentle voice what was the matter with the little girl.

Willie whipped off his cap, and in his quiet, precise manner told the lady just what had happened, and added:

"I don't think she's really hurt, ma'am, but just scared, that's all. I'm only afraid she'll catch cold going home in those wet things."

"She must not go home till they have been dried. Here, bring her up to my house and I will take care of her," said the lady kindly. With his heart beating with a very turmoil of emotions Willie hurried his sister up to the cottage, where the lady took them into a cozy kitchen.

It was prettily decorated with blue and white china, with dainty curtains to the latticed windows and quaint little seats on either side of a large open fireplace in which there were sticks and logs laid ready for lighting. Hastily putting a match to the fire, the lady began to take off the child's wet clothes, and while doing so she said to Willie:

"I will call my little boy and tell him to go down with you to the brook. I don't generally allow him to associate with the children about here, but I see you are a well-brought up child and you may play together. Don't trouble about your little sister. I will take care of her."

So a few minutes later the two boys were fishing happily together beside the stream, while the lady rubbed the little girl into a glow with warm, dry cloths, and then put her to bed with a hot water bottle to her feet, and after giving her a nice warm drink, bade her go to sleep while her clothes were drying.

Willie soon ascertained that the boy's name was Arthur, that he was about his own age and that he had lost his papa. Further than that the little fellow was not communicative and our hero was far too diplomatic to ply him with questions. He felt quite sure that this so-called Mrs. Smith was the long-lost Mrs. Ferris, and his chief desire was in no way to arouse her suspicions as to his knowing anything about the doctor. He was in an agony lest Polly should let out anything, but he need not have feared, for his sister was fast asleep in the old-fashioned four-post bedstead, and she only awoke when Mrs. Smith called her to get up and dress in her nice dry things, all beautifully ironed out and as dainty as when she had put them on that morning.

Then the lady called the two boys and said that she thought they would like a cup of tea before they started home. She took them into a pretty parlor, full of beautiful pictures and dainty knick-knacks, and gave them tea out of such beautiful china cups that Willie was almost afraid to take hold of his.

He was profuse in his thanks and expressions of gratitude, and Mrs. Smith told him that she would be very glad to have them come and play with Arthur any afternoon, so long as they came alone.

The old farmers' astonishment knew no bounds when they heard that the two children had been admitted into the mysterious cottage, and they never tired of making Willie and his little sister relate all the details of this wonderful adventure of theirs.

Chapter XIV
Found at Last!

Much as Willie enjoyed every minute of his time at the farm, and of the afternoons with Arthur, he felt as if he never could live through the intervening days until the doctor should arrive. At night he could hardly sleep for excitement.

He had warned Polly not to say a word about Dr. Ferris and not to know anything if she was asked. He had even taken the cousins into his confidence a little bit, for he felt the slightest indiscretion might spoil everything.

On the very eve of the day he was expecting the doctor, Mrs. Smith asked him how he was going home.

"I suppose your cousin is going to drive you to the station?" she said.

"Well, you see, I could hardly walk so far," said Willie with his merry smile.

"You live in San Francisco, don't you?"

"Yes, ma'am," answered Willie, whose heart began to thump.

"Oh!" said Mrs. Smith in a voice she tried to make very indifferent, "I heard that an old friend of mine, Dr. Ferris, was living there. Did you ever hear of a doctor with that name?"

Willie saw his sister start, and gave her a vigorous nudge under the table, as he answered coolly:

"Ferris? Dr. Ferris? Well, I may have heard the name, but there's such heaps and heaps of doctors in San Francisco that one can't remember them all. They say there's more than one doctor for every day in the year in our city."

The lady looked at him very hard as he spoke, but she could not detect the slightest hesitation in his answer.

"Oh! I see," she continued in the same indifferent tone. "I thought you might have heard his name mentioned some time, that's all."

The next day Willie sent his sister alone to the cottage under pretext that his leg was aching, and cousin Sam drove him by another way to the crossroads where he was sure to see the doctor coming in his automobile.

The child leaned against a tree by the roadside, and it seemed to him as if the auto would never appear. After a time he paced up and down, and then said his rosary. Finally, to his intense joy, he noticed a cloud of dust on the road, and soon saw the doctor waving to him.

Poor Willie was so frantic with excitement that he could hardly speak, but made the doctor stop the auto under the shadow of a tree while he told his story. Then it was agreed that they should leave the car by the roadside and walk quietly up to the house. The doctor dreaded lest the child should be mistaken, but Willie was positive of the resemblance of the lady and child to the portraits, and with beating hearts they approached the house. Willie knocked at the door, calling very ungrammatically, "It's me, Willie!"

The door opened and the child said quietly, "I've brought a friend."

There was a cry of "Miriam! At last! At last I've

The child leaned against a tree by the roadside... Finally, to his intense joy, he noticed a cloud of dust on the road, and soon saw the doctor waving to him.

found you!" but Willie heard no more, for with a dexterous sweep of his crutch he hopped outside again and closed the door behind him.

After what seemed an age to him the door opened and the doctor smilingly beckoned him in.

"Oh, you little schemer!" laughed the lady, shaking her finger at him, "I little knew I was entertaining a private detective."

"And one who has accomplished what hundreds of others failed to do," laughed the doctor.

"Oh, I did not accomplish anything," said Willie. "You know that was my First Holy Communion prayer. God was sure to help us find them after that. Are you angry with me?" he added, looking up into the lady's beautiful face.

"No, I'm far too happy to be angry. It seems too silly! But I've been hiding all this while, I think, longing to be found!"

And now that all our friends are happy, what can we do better but leave them to their thankful joy? Even Willie's lame leg the doctors hope to be able to cure completely in time, and, if God grants him this, the child has a great, great wish, which Dr. Ferris has promised to give him the means to carry out. Surely I need not tell you what it is? You can guess it for yourselves.

"Oh, I do hope, I do hope the good Jesus will grant me my wish," said Willie wistfully one day. Then with his brave smile he added, "But if He doesn't, I feel sure that anyhow He'll let me work for Him in some way or other."

And those who know how much good has already been done by the "Little Apostle on Crutches" feel not the slightest doubt about the matter. In some way or other Willie will always work for his dear Master.